THE SOWING AND THE REAPING

THE SOWING AND THE REAPING

by

GEORGE STEWART

The CAXTON PRINTERS, Ltd.
Caldwell, Idaho
1970

International Standard Book Number 0-87004-200-9

Library of Congress Catalog Card No. 71-109540

Printed and bound in the United States of America by
The CAXTON PRINTERS, Ltd.
Caldwell, Idaho 83605
113309

TO LENI

CONTENTS

PART I
COLORADO
In which I Endeavor To Become a Rancher's Boy

OUR ranch on Minnesota Creek was a remnant of large holdings my father once had owned in the North Fork of the Gunnison. After he endured much hardship in the lead and zinc diggings in Southwest Missouri, some good mines came in, enabling him to realize a long-held goal to buy ranches in Colorado.

Affairs did not go too well for my parents in those years in their life together. They were able, had vision, and could take punishment, but they were not a team, and when I was very young, they were divorced. Mother was a wild child of the prairie, impulsive, generous, with a marked capacity to win friends, to enjoy them, to serve them well, and never to lose them. She grew to be a woman of iron whims, with a fair amount of false pride, not too good an organizer, nevertheless she put behind her solid accomplishments of which she could have justifiably boasted.

My father was close-knit in body and mind, not much given to talk, openhanded, with a fine sense of order, never a complainer, and a beaver for work. He was a realist, uninterested in pride not based on genuine prowess, and he deeply cherished family honor. Having been reared in the school of hard knocks, he was accustomed to poverty as well as to riches. He accepted pain, loss, and hard luck as native to life.

When money became plentiful before he and mother were divorced, he purchased thirteen ranches on the Western Slope, a region familiar to him from having prospected there in earlier days. It was during this period of prosperity that tension developed between my parents, leading to the family breakup. Father subsequently remarried.

We children stayed with Mother, most of the time in Baxter Springs, Kansas, just over the line from Missouri, and the Indian Territory. Father had provided a house for us and an agreed-upon amount of money, but in a few years misfortune overtook him in the mines, forcing him to discontinue payments. Mother understood and never complained, turning to sewing, keeping boarders, clerking, and various other jobs to support us. She made men's shirts, if they furnished the material, for fifty cents each, buttonholes and all. We may have been ill housed, ill fed, ill clothed, but we never knew it. We were always broke—but never poor.

There were four children to care for: my brother Clifford, untimely dead in early childhood, my sisters Nell and Anne, and I. My sisters were consistent readers, always near the top of their classes, known for their good taste and their unusual knowledge of antiques. In later years Nell had several collections pictured and described in magazines and shown in various museums. Both girls finished high school to take positions as teachers. I rank Nell as the best teacher I ever had, clever in instruction, developing in pupils a relish for learning, and a strict disciplinarian. My sister Anne also developed exceptional qualities as a teacher and was much in demand. As soon as they began earning, both generously helped with family expenses. Later Anne studied at Mount Holyoke College and graduated from the University of Kansas.

Baxter Springs had everything we could desire. There were numerous relatives, self-reliant, eager that children should receive a sound education, good neighbors and, in general, prosperous. And there were wide prairies, Indians of a dozen nations nearby in the Territory only a mile away, who did their trading in our stores. There were rivers and creeks for swimming, boating and fishing, forests for persimmons, paw paws, May apples, sassafras, nuts, and wild grapes. We had also the magnificent, yearly Old

Soldiers' Reunion, with hundreds of Confederate and Union veterans in Gray and Blue uniforms for a week of parades, speeches and family gatherings; and we had also our unique Tin Money Towns every summer. There was good deer hunting not far away, an abundance of rabbits, doves and quail, and above all excellent schools to make life rich, full and exciting for the young ones.

When Father bought his ranches in Colorado, before his financial cyclone struck, he promptly turned his hand to building an irrigation system leading to a mesa which bears his name. The head of the canal, which carried 2,200 miners' inches of water, was on a raging tributary of the Colorado. Various engineers were associated with him in the project but he furnished the ideas, the will, and the money to put the work through under his personal supervision. Today it is still called the Stewart Ditch Company.

The irrigation system began forty-five miles from a railroad. Materials for a seven-hundred-foot flume had to be hauled across country, four-horse-team loads of three-inch tongue-and-groove lumber. On its course the big ditch passed along steep mountainsides for many miles. A path had to be shoveled out first to furnish foothold for a single horse. An animal called Buckskin Jimmie, a resolute, fearless gelding of the breed now called Palomino, picked his way along this slender track with a light plow until a sufficient way was made for a four-horse plow to operate. At intervals a platform was built out over the mountainside so that when the outfit arrived at that spot the horses could pick their way around to make the return trip. It was ticklish work, and not all of it could be done by horses, plows, and scrapers. One section of several hundred yards was tough adobe soil mixed with dolomite boulders. No plow could uproot these, they turned the points of the hardest steel drills. In this locality it was pick, shovel, dynamite, and human brawn. Years later Father built a tunnel for this section of the canal, directly through the backbone of the mountain.

Many accidents happened: infections of hands, broken

limbs, and horses falling down the mountainside. One huge bay rolled three hundred feet head over heels into the boiling, yellow river, got up, shook himself, and scrambled up the mountain to the feeding pens. A magnificent string of some eighty horses was employed for this work, Percherons and Belgian crossbreeds, patient and sagacious beasts, not easily rattled.

Some of these draft horses had almost too much sense. After the ditch was finished a splendid horse called John decided to retire. He was a big dapple-gray, well fed, apparently with no reason to complain, but he nevertheless decided to quit work. All ordinary means were used to persuade him. Sand was put into his mouth to distract his attention, to no avail. He was whipped but refused to tighten a tug. He was through working. My father, understanding that there was no use abusing him, suspecting that some careless driver had made him balky, turned him out of the corral of working horses. From then on John led the life of a dilletante. He was a kindly soul, standing in well with farm girls who helped in the ranch kitchen. Daily he collected offerings from them in the way of apples and various tidbits. He ate anything—plums, dried fruit, biscuits, honey and even custard pie. Once the girls gave him a piece of spiced bologna. Insulted, he turned his backside and nearly kicked the kitchen loose from the rambling ranch house. Dishes flew all over and crashed to the floor. Hard-working ranch hands took pleasure in watching this huge lout of a horse taking his ease. He loafed out to fields where other horses were slaving, dug his Roman nose into their ribs in contempt for honest toil, and even lay down to watch them. At haying time he superintended stacking from the shade of a peach tree, surreptitiously drinking up small barrels of water brought out for the thirsty men. He ransacked lunch pails with the thoroughness of a magpie.

John often followed my father on his daily trip to the village of Paonia but would soon tire of the rapid gait of the driving horses and pause to eat wisps of alfalfa along the way. Thirty minutes later he would saunter into town, where he was well known. There he would visit cronies in the blacksmith's shop. One time as he meandered down the boardwalk he broke through as a boy would on thin ice. The splintered boards formed a trap but he waited patiently while the deputy sheriff sawed him out.

A splendid black Percheron mare named Cal lived on our ranch until she was thirty-five, a noble animal frequently used in training colts. In later years when I visited France I took special interest in horses of the La Perce region bordering the plain of La Beauce, of which Chartres is the capital. This corner of France was immortalized by Emile Zola's *La Terre*. I saw many horses there which reminded me of old Cal.

Overexpansion in the mines brought financial trouble which soon lost Father his ranches and his stock in the irrigation system. A few years later he regained his Minnesota Creek Ranch and it was there I joined him and my stepmother. I came presumably for a summer, but it did not turn out that way.

Soil on the Minnesota Creek ranch was rich, but the cultivated fields were largely undeveloped and badly neglected. Many acres lay in old beaver dams where oak brush, red birch, willows, and aspens were so tangled that it was impossible for a man to pass. Fences were down and fields were defenseless against attacks of savage range cattle. We were compelled to build heavy fences with birch poles wired upon them. Then came clearing for new land, and on one section near the mountain, an endless amount of rock picking. We gathered over three-hundred wagonloads of stones from less than twelve acres. This ranch had an indifferent orchard of some twenty acres.

Father never pitied himself, he had been rich, now he was poor. Without complaint he swung his axe week after week in grim winter weather and the clearings grew. In the spring, fires were set to rid the land of slashings. A mixture of oat and alfalfa seed was disked in, for heavy roots made plowing impossible. By midsummer there was a knee-deep growth of alfalfa and oats, together with oak, rose briar, and willow sprouts. We cut it while the sprouts were still tender and fed it to the stock.

Before Father was twenty he had driven a six-horse team from Omaha to Denver. From there he joined another wagon train headed for Cripple Creek, and later worked at Leadville. With little formal schooling he nevertheless persisted until he became a first-class mining engineer, often traveling long distances to appraise mines in Alaska, Mexico, and the Western states.

During the winter of 1879-80 he had carried the mail on skis over the pass from Alpine to Tincup in Colorado. High pay was given for any extras, a dollar for a spool of thread or an old newspaper, five dollars for a plug of tobacco, ten dollars for a quart of whiskey. A giant Negro made the trip with him every other day with a pack of flour, bacon, or condensed foods for the Gold Cup mine. Both were well armed for there were still hostile Indians about and not infrequently road agents. Father had three notches on his six shooter but never discussed them.

For a year in the early eighties Father had hunted meat, mostly bear, deer, and grouse, for miners of Aspen, Colorado. He did every sort of work connected with mining operations. Gradually he became an accomplished chemist, a builder of mills, crushers and jigs, and an expert in pumps and ventilation. He held his own with geologists who read the cataclysmic jumble of strata in the Rockies like an open book. He sat on Vigilante Committees and acted as midwife in prospectors' cabins during his initiation into the Western fraternity, he froze in wet blankets, spent weeks in unexplored mountains seeking new veins, shared his grub with anyone who was needy, and drank his share of whiskey.

In Baxter Springs life had been varied: camping, fishing, gathering nuts and wild fruit, swimming in season, no regular daily work, rambling about with relatives and schoolmates, and going down into the Territory to visit Indian friends. On the Minnesota Creek ranch it was entirely different, and my first summer there was the hardest, my father and stepmother worked hard from dawn to dusk, and I worked hard at rock picking, irrigating, and chores with the animals. No other boy lived within several miles and I met none until I started school in the autumn. As the summer weeks went by I grew homesick for Baxter Springs and the easier and exciting life of small adventures with my cousins, my mother, generous sisters, and the Indians. Especially did I miss the two crowning events of our summers, the Tin Money Towns and the Old Soldiers' Reunions.

Tin Money Towns had been developed in great elaboration among boys and girls with whom I played. We mashed metal caps of beer bottles upon our mothers' flatirons, sometimes ruining the irons in the process. These metal tokens we employed as money, with an equivalent for all coins we knew, both gold and silver. Champagne metal caps, being a bit more elaborate, were used as ten- and twenty-dollar gold pieces.

We kept a bank, various stores, and places of amusement. Prices in our town, as prices everywhere, depended upon the amount of money in circulation. Economists would have had little trouble convincing us regarding the quantity theory of money. When beer-bottle caps ran low they bought a great deal, and prices went down. When someone discovered a new supply, prices went up, and money was cheap. Money was a commodity, not an absolute standard by divine right. One boy went on a holiday to Joplin, Missouri, a few miles away. He gathered up half a gunnysack of metal caps back of the long row of saloons. When he returned a veritable panic occurred. Prices skyrocketed. He and his sister, like profiteers in Germany during the inflation, bought up everything in sight. We held an emergency cabinet meeting to revaluate the currency, even as our elders did later.

We sold everything; that is, everything we could persuade our mothers to give us, or that was not under lock and key. In our mart one could purchase dogs, cats, rabbits, birds' eggs, both fresh and blown, feathers, green apples, melons, cooked food and portions of home meals that we stole and hid in our clothing. I bought one of the best cats I ever had from the lawyer's son for twenty beer-bottle tins and a champagne top.

There were also various drinks. Boys, well versed in illegal liquor selling in our presumably dry territory, ran "blind tigers" in which tea and coffee, the remains in old medicine bottles, and various vinegary mixtures were sold. A kindly Providence smiled upon us, for none of us died from poisoning. I did have a badly swollen hand from spilling carbolic acid on it from a bottle which I was taking to my sister's store to sell for perfume. A policeman and a jail with appropriate fines and sentences were provided for those who broke the code of our towns. Big boys always grabbed this job and made a lot of money out of it.

Gambling was a prominent feature. We had roulette wheels, dice, and cards. Some of the older children were quite expert in playing steal casino, pitch, pinochle, and even poker, and all of us boys were experienced crap shooters. Prizes were given for those who could hit targets with bow and arrows or air rifles.

Special costumes were worn; the boys made use of cast-off trousers of fathers and elder brothers. Derby hats were at a premium; walking sticks were affected; stiff-bosomed shirts were considered a prize. One lad had an old-fashioned silk tile, while girls fancied mantillas made of lace curtains and puffed sleeves worn by mothers. Gay silk underskirts, fans, and black silk mitts were brought from storage closets and attics. Our narrow streets did not lack color.

In late August when the Old Soldiers' Reunion was taking place back in Kansas, the dreadfully homesick boy that I was, I recalled details of those wonderful weeks, the fine meals with relatives, stirring parades, and the ringing voices of veterans.

At the Old Soldiers' Reunions, Grand Army and Confederate veterans from a radius of two hundred and fifty miles gathered for ten days to renew old friendships, to fight Civil War campaigns over again in speeches and parades. There were special gatherings of regiments and participants in various battles. Hundreds rented tents and took families to the reunion grounds. There were perhaps at least fifty cases where one brother had gone with Grant and another with Lee.

Fakirs of every sort, snake charmers, gamblers, bootleggers, prostitutes, and amusement companies with hootchie-kootchie dancers flocked to the scene. Down in the woods an improvised saloon was opened, strictly against the law, but no one dared raise an objection. On rough pine counters were rows of pints and quarts of fiery, cheap whiskey, and thousands of bottles of beer. Indians waited on the outskirts of the crowd. It was a Federal offense to sell liquor to Government wards or for their white neighbors to give it to them. Nevertheless, every Red brave procured firewater. Old soldiers indulged heartily; one saw a veteran of Antietam or Lookout Mountain stretched upon the earth, or, in his tent, while good-natured relatives waited for him to sober up. The sheriff and his deputies were busy after pickpockets and thieves, but culprits who sold illegal liquor were never touched. Once I followed a deputy, a man with a long list of killings in behalf of the law, one of the best two-hand gunmen of the Southwest, right through the center of this great liquor den to seize a wretched man who had stolen a bicycle. Men drinking at the bar stood, glasses in hands, and congratulated the officer as he walked off to the calaboose with his catch. The breach of certain laws was an accepted convention. Once during a reunion a group of us boys bought a gallon jug of whiskey through an older friend and became very drunk.

Sunrise and sunset guns and full military pomp were observed throughout the Reunion encampments. On a certain day at each Reunion a roll call was made by regiments and states. Loudest cheers always awaited sole responders from distant states, such as Vermont or Massachusetts. Old battle flags were unfurled, grey-haired sons often supported white-haired fathers as they marched in the parades, old loyalties were burnished, old swords brandished, old friendships renewed. Long lines of relatives and friends cheered and wept and sang with marching veterans. These were people who came across the Alleghenies in prairie schooners, who saved Kansas and Missouri to the Union, who were the followers of John Brown at Ossowatamie, who bled on all the great battlefields of the South.

Hundreds were present in gray uniform of the Confederacy. One saw aged warriors who had fought each other at Bull Run and Cold Harbor, walking arm in arm, drinking from the same bottle, their families dining together under oak trees as though the Civil War had never happened. On days when Confederates paraded with their flag snapping beside the Stars and Stripes, men in blue stood hat in hand and cheered former enemies until they were voiceless. This was Border country.

On that first hard summer in Colorado I fed on memories of Kansas and the Indian Territory. As I moved about the ranch, becoming used to new jobs, animals, sights, and smells, full of homesickness and self pity, vivid scenes of the old soldiers were constantly with me, for they combined all my ideas of patriotism and our people's history. One Confederate colonel returned each year, a cavalryman. The left sleeve of his spotless gray uniform was empty. With his big hat, his insignia, the bright *sabre tache,* the long sword he used in his salute to both the Stars and Bars and the Stars and Stripes, a long red scar across his face, his trimmed gray beard, his erect figure astride a handsome bay horse, he was the very spit and image of a hero. As these aging men, marched in perfect order, remnants of divisions and regiments, they joined in old battle songs, both North and South: "Tenting on the Old Camp Ground," "The Battle Hymn of the Republic," "Oh! Suzanna!," "The Yellow Rose of Texas," "Dixie," "Maryland, My Maryland," "Yankee Doodle," "Tramp, Tramp, Tramp," "John Brown's

Body," "We Are Coming, Father Abraham," and "When Johnny Comes Marching Home."

The Northerners would cheer "Dixie" as loudly as the rebels, and the southern veterans would sing along as Yankees made the forest vibrate with "Marching Through Georgia." The singing was wonderful, and we youngsters knew every verse of every song.

Long evenings at the Old Soldiers' Reunions provided a setting for family gatherings, impromptu sing fests and recitations. Veterans and friends moved from tent to tent enjoying food and drink, without specific invitations, for it was open house the entire week. One solo often sung, dating from the war, was, "Lorena." Barbershop quartets made the rounds while children were often asked to speak pieces. Three times at one reunion I heard a much invited, beautiful girl recite Finch's, "The Blue and The Gray." Later I found it in a book at school, and I never forgot it.

By the flow of the inland river,
Whence the fleets of iron have fled;
Where the blades of the grave-grass quiver,
Asleep are the ranks of the dead:
  Under the sod and the dew,
    Waiting the judgment day;
  Under the one, the Blue,
    Under the other, the Gray.

These in the robings of glory,
Those in the gloom of defeat,
All with the battle-blood gory,
In the dusk of eternity meet:
  Under the sod and the dew,
    Waiting the judgment day;
  Under the laurel, the Blue,
    Under the willow, the Gray.

Sadly, but not with upbraiding,
The generous deed was done,
In the storm of the years that are fading
No braver battle was won:
  Under the sod and the dew,
    Waiting the judgment day;
  Under the blossoms, the Blue,
    Under the garlands, the Gray.

No more shall the war cry sever,
Or the winding rivers be red;
They banish our anger forever
When they laurel the graves of our dead!
Under the sod and the dew,
Waiting the judgment day;
Love and tears for the Blue,
Tears and love for the Gray.

This last verse was eventually carved on the Civil War Memorial at Yale.

Were we sentimentalists? Yes, unashamedly so, cherishing patriotism, kinfolk, neighbors, and all that had to do with our land and its people. These families, renewing friendships, seeing relatives, and reliving stirring events, had known hardship and danger, and would continue so to do. In one sense, they were celebrating together some measure of victory in their struggle and were being fed by some inward nourishment, faith in one another and in the nation, a faith which reinforced them for hard tomorrows—faith, the most vital factor in our collective life. In spite of Northern carpetbaggers and injustices imposed on the South, there was never a civil war, or any war, where most participants on opposing sides so quickly achieved mutual respect and forgiveness, a spiritual reconciliation, immediately begun by Grant and Lee at Appomatox. Some, of course, were never able to accept defeat, or victory.

Most of us children had had one, or both, grandfathers in uniform, in many cases on opposite sides. We came to see, to learn, to partake, and to remember. We, too, were fed by a ghostly nourishment and, in our small way, were able "to walk in the strength of that food for forty days and forty nights." The Reunions added a dimension to our lives. Time, with increasing rapidity, mowed down the ranks of these veterans.

We young ones did not clearly understand reasons for the Civil War. We loved the Blue and the Gray equally, we loved our land, and we loved these fine men. Although in our school we were almost all from Union families, never was a word said against some boy or girl whose father or grandfather had worn the uniform of the Confederacy.

No matter how sorry I felt for myself in this first, strange, hardest summer on Minnesota Creek, or how difficult and long the work, my feet and hands moved faster when I fed on these bright memories.

Gradually I made the change from a life of casual chores and unorganized days, and my body grew hard, my hands skillful, and with this came an acceptance of teamwork, long days, and purposeful labor for a far-off harvest. From a mood of silent rebellion, I dimly began to develop an ambition to become a competent ranch hand.

One stormy night there was a big racket outside. My father thought someone was attempting to break into the house. He picked up his Winchester and went outdoors, but it turned out to be only some coyotes seeking food. Before I could settle down to sleep again many scenes of my childhood flitted in and out of my mind. I remembered one glacial night in Baxter Springs when a burglar broke into my mother's home. Mother got up, lit a lamp, and called in a loud voice to my elder sister, "Nell, bring that revolver under your pillow. I have my six-shooter. Someone has broken into the house. Follow me down. Shoot to kill." She sailed by the door of my room in her nightgown, lamp in hand, with Nell after her. Both made their way down the stairway in bare feet, hair flying. The burglar left through an open window. Mother gloated over her triumph that night; she'd had no guns and had bluffed!

She then soothed us with stories of Jesse James, Cole Younger, the Dalton gang, and other border brigands. One yarn I remember was about the famous woman outlaw Belle Starr. Clothed as a man, Belle was accommodated one night at a hotel which customarily asked strange guests to share a double bed with another person. Early the next morning, she arose, dressed, strapped on her gun belt and awakened her companion who was still snoring. "Mister," she said, "when you get home tell your wife you have had the honor of sleeping with Belle Starr!" After much talk

Mother drank several cups of black coffee and went to sleep. Next day she bought an Iver Johnson revolver to keep under her pillow.

A niece of my stepmother, who had lost her parents, came to live with us on the ranch. She was a magnificent young woman who later graduated from the State University at Fort Collins. Some years later my father wrote to inquire if I had any objections if she were adopted into the family, and of course I was favorable. Later she married a professor, the two having had a very fruitful life at a college in Vermont.

Geologists, miners, and cattlemen who came to us on visits were a hardy lot, and their women were not one whit behind them. As far as I know my Aunt Mary was the first white woman to cross the Continental Divide on snowshoes, venturing hundreds of miles from any settlement, prospecting with her husband and my father in search of gold, going clear out to the Moab Valley in Utah. Once they found two horse thieves hanging from a tree near the Green River in eastern Utah. As their own boots were nearly gone they exchanged with the dead men.

From time to time a visitor would show up unannounced whom Father had not seen for years, and they were always welcome. There were hours of reminiscences which I drank in, adventures, hardships, lucky strikes, successes and failures. Men sometimes stayed with us as long as six months, helping in the work if needed. In many ways they brought in the larger airs of the outside world, and they certainly enlarged my horizon.

Mount Gunnison, retaining snowfields and small glaciers even in hottest summers, was the source of Minnesota Creek and was among the higher peaks in Colorado. It was not visible from our ranch, as the valley of Minnesota Creek is narrow and deep. But on higher places the full grandeur stood out against the sky. To the west, however, the mass of Red Mountain overlooked the whole countryside and, still farther westward across the deep valley of the North Fork of the Gunnison River, it dominated a vast expanse on Grand Mesa, a land of high parks and lakes, then completely uninhabited, a range for cattle and a refuge for creatures of the wild.

In geologic times Red Mountain had been thrust up through a series of old lake beds, with dozens of strata of red sandstone, alternating with layers of softer substances of lighter color, which wind, frost, and water had eroded, often deeply undermining harder sandstone which through the years had broken off in immense blocks. Fossils were found there but we children knew little of distant ages from whence they came. Occasionally one saw fossil specimens in stone or coal at ranch houses but there was sparse curiosity about such matters. Lower down, shales, decomposed over centuries, gave way to adobe stretches on which grew thousands of scrub cedars. Wedged between various strata were frequent beds of coal of good quality.

Colors were vivid—reds, pinks, yellows, blues, purples, and browns, changing perpetually during days of sunshine and in different seasons of the year.

In softer strata, animals enlarged holes eroded by the weather. Squirrels, bobcats, and prairie dogs found homes there, and a number of bears. Bees stored honey in these openings, far more than their winter's needs. Summer heat often melted these caches, the honey running down in a viscous mass. Bears loved honey, making perilous climbs to raid the hoards. Some honey was aged black, becoming inedible; other deposits suffered from disease.

Red Mountain was a lonely and silent place. Grass was so thin few cattle fed there. In the dry chaos of fallen stone beneath cliffs rattlesnakes made their abode, while eagles had nests and a refuge in high solitudes toward the summit. Hawks and magpies frequented lower slopes; robins, meadowlarks, and smaller birds lived only in more pleasant places in the valley.

It was not a green or handsome mountain, but it did have a sullen austere majesty, the most distinctive natural feature of our restricted region. We boys who hunted there generally went in pairs, for the voiceless land could be a region of fear and trepidation.

During my years on the creek we were so hard pressed with work that I went only once for a few days up to the foot of Mount Gunnison. There were plenty of rabbits in the sage, while bobcats frequented the scrub cedar belt. A neighbor shot forty-two in one winter.

Beyond Red Mountain, but part of the same geological mass, was Fire Mountain, which had a conflagration going on in its bowels, perhaps for centuries. It could have been started by lightning, by Indian cooking fires, or by forest fires. Such phenomena occur in a number of coal-mining areas. The miners at Somerset at the foot of Fire Mountain occasionally run into burnt-out veins. No blazes are apparent but near the top of Fire Mountain smoke and gases emerge.

Spring was the best season of the year in our valley. For a short period desert land bloomed with primroses, violets, buttercups, black-eyed Susans, cowslips, and dozens of varieties of small plants which were soon cut down by the scorching sun. I have never heard meadowlarks with so sweet a song as there. Magpies, handsome and saucy, were great robbers around the barns. We must have been on one of the migratory bird routes for I saw many in spring and autumn which did not summer with us. Over our valley floated the smell of sage and cedar in the clean mountain air.

When summer ended I decided to stay on with my father. I never went back to my mother's home.

While on Minnesota Creek I witnessed a magnificent cloudburst. Water streamed from the sky, raindrops were scarcely distinguishable. When the storm suddenly stopped, opposite our ranch on Red Mountain torrents roared down carrying boulders which bounded high in the air, sometimes splitting by centrifugal force, smashing trees into kindling wood. Minnesota Creek rose rapidly, the water thick with mud. It overflowed all our bottomland

and proved a blessing. Heavy silt leveled up old beaver holes and inequalities, leaving a rich deposit of mud.

Those who live in mountainous country see the grandeur of storms at their most majestic moments. The valley of Minnesota Creek was narrow into which came canyon-like tributaries, with high mountains on either side. When lightning played over the landscape, the crash of thunder echoing back and forth for long periods was akin to a full-scale bombardment of large caliber guns. Storms were awesome and frightening to man and beast.

Each autumn I attended Dry Gulch School in our small alpine valley. It was a tiny, poorly made frame building in an exposed spot. In early fall and spring the heat was intolerable in the schoolhouse. In winter it was a target for biting winds. Nearly forty of us, in one room, had a single teacher, a tall, rawboned young Missourian without college training, but determined to educate himself as well as his pupils. Each noon hour he ate lunch in fifteen minutes and spent the remainder of the time on his studies. A week after he started work a fight broke out, the stove was upset, and the children panicked. The teacher promptly knocked down two of the older boys who had started the ruckus and we had good discipline after that.

In the few hours of the school day our teacher had eighteen classes including primary through eighth grade. It was an inhuman task to place on any educator, but he did it. In a month he had little tots reading and writing, carrying on all other work with the same facility. On Saturdays he worked ten hours on ranches for a dollar and a half a day. Of the boys and girls who were in that school when I attended it, ten have university degrees. A pair of twin boys worked their way through college at Fort Collins to become two of the best veterinarians on the Western Slope.

Discipline at Dry Gulch was stern but just. For one thrashing I received at the hands of the young teacher, I was compelled to cut a bundle of skunk brush limbs which he then used on me until there was nothing left in his hand with which to whip me. I could hardly sit down for a week.

In spring the school board met to decide policies, to elect the teacher, and to fix up the schoolhouse. Yellowhammers, woodpeckers, and squirrels had bored holes in the walls of the schoolhouse building nests of frayed cedar bark on the inside. The school board members mashed out lard pails into flat sheets and nailed them over these holes. In time the building was plastered all over with these tin badges. Now and then a yellowhammer would light on one of these patches during school time to start his staccato beat which reverberated like a machine gun. We children sniggered and twisted at the familiar sound. Another diversion was the sonorous braying of burros which several pupils rode to school and tied to a long hitching rack. Children made blankets of gunnysacks or canvas from old tents to cover the burros in stormy weather, for they loved them.

Noon hour was the climax of the day as everyone brought lunch. Older children were allowed coffee which was poured into a common pail to be heated on the stove in the center of the room. The schoolmaster ate with us, often trading food—a slice of pie for a sandwich. He drank coffee out of the same pail with the children. There were games of pullaway, tag, and follow-the-leader over rugged hillsides, or snowball wars with forts. Best of all was bobsledding over a half-mile course with a sharp bend in it which required expert steering. Each winter there were broken bones but the games were worth the pain.

The teacher was skillful in arranging contests in what we called mental arithmetic, simple problems in addition, division, multiplication, and subtraction. Many children learned the multiplication table, not only to the usual twelve times twelve, but up to twenty. The best fun was the spelling bees. Every boy and girl would test out others as we walked home, and later our parents.

It was common practice then for teachers to impress on the minds of their students certain short poems or paragraphs from patriotic or other utterances of men and women in public life. The teacher wrote this on the blackboard the first day of school, and I never forgot the words:

Work for some good
Be it ever so slowly.
Cherish some flower
Be it ever so lowly
For labor, all labor
Is noble and holy.

There were also verses of Scripture such as, "Thy shoes shall be iron and brass, and as thy days so shall thy strength be," or, "Be thou faithful unto death, and I will give thee the crown of life."

It could be that we lived too much on these old mottoes and aphorisms. Country people everywhere are prone to proverbs. We heard them at home and our teacher put them on the blackboard. He probably picked them up on his father's farm. There was one each day such as: A spoonful of honey attracts more flies than a quart of vinegar. Little people should have long ears, but short tongues. Borrowing is the scissors of friendship. He who can walk has a good horse. Fool me once, shame on you, fool me twice, shame on me. If two men ride the same horse one man must ride in front. A half a loaf is better than no bread. Two swallows do not make a spring. Save the pennies and the dollars will take care of themselves. A fool and his money soon part. One rotten apple spoils a whole barrel. No need for the pot to call the kettle black. People in glass houses should not throw stones. An empty kettle makes the loudest noise. If you aim at two rabbits, you miss both. Painted flowers have no smell. A stream rises no higher than its source.

Our teacher would read off his daily proverb, write it on the blackboard, make a practical application close to home with a few salty remarks, never labor the matter, and pass on to the long series of classes. Old shibboleths, bromides, slogans, perhaps, but they lingered in our minds to guide us at moments when we were too tired or confused to think. Most great truths can be stated in platitudes which can be remembered.

The boys at Dry Gulch School badly needed a catcher's

glove but no one had the needed two dollars and a half. Teacher and mothers collaborated arranging a box supper to raise the money. The girls used shoe boxes, placing in them delicious cold food—chicken, ham, sandwiches, pickles, preserves, fruit, cake, all sorts of good things. These boxes were wrapped in fancy paper and tied with a ribbon. All were auctioned off on the night selected when nothing sold for more than fifty cents, but we raised enough not only to buy the catcher's glove, but also several bats. I bid on what I thought was the box of a pretty girl, but the owner turned out to be her homely sister.

No boy ever had a whole suit of clothes, as cold weather came we put on another pair of overalls. A great boon was to have an old, heavy mackinaw of our fathers. We liked very much the long sleeves as they helped warm our hands. A pair of new shoes was admired by everyone. There were no complaints about new shoes squeaking, we rejoiced in it! If a pupil rose to get a drink of water from the pail in the corner, all eyes were upon him as he walked, taking care that every squeak was audible.

We had a lot of music in our school. In addition to pieces in our music books, we all learned songs of the land such as "Remember the Red River Valley." One song began:

Young man you're a robber
You'd better take it fair
Leave off your stealing
And live upon the square
If you meet a fine horse
Just pass him by,
Travel on your muscle boys,
Root, hog, or die!

The young Missouri teacher was almost as good an instructor as my sister Nell whose classes I had attended in Baxter Springs. I told him about Nell's method of teaching geography which he copied to the advantage of everyone.

Nell, in her geography classes, had required us to trace

ships from port to port around the world by the most difficult passages she could devise, and had us lade them with products of lands they touched. Under her guidance we traded copra, lumber, and spices from Malaysia for New Zealand mutton or Manchester cotton. Every girl and boy in her classes could navigate a ship from Vladivostok to Kronstadt through all intervening straits and seas before passing her course. We traded in hides, gums, coffee, silk, hemp, tea, ebony, teak, nitrates, gems, livestock, wild animals, wheat, and dates in every port from Antafogasta to Perim, and we made the exchange of money, giving her a final accounting in U.S. dollars.

This money exchange business was not too difficult for currencies were more or less stable in those days. Almanacs had tables showing values of moneys throughout the world.

One girl in the Dry Gulch School ran out of imagination when her 10,000-ton freighter docked in Manila. She loaded the entire vessel with Rhesus monkeys, hundreds of the shocking little pests. Why did we not descend from elephants, lions, or raccoons, instead of these mocking, noisome, talkative, stinking, arrogant creatures? We would have, as a group, amounted to far more.

Anyway, as the little girl's freighter quit Singapore and was passing the Malacca Straits, she became worried about disposal of her merchandise. At Calcutta she gave away one hundred of her monkeys. This practice she continued in port after port, finally arriving at Galveston with an even dozen. These she presented to her classmates. How she proposed to deliver them was not reported. But what of profits? She faced reality. Her father helped her estimate the cost of coal, provisions, and pay for the crew. She reported a loss of $15,000 for the operation. On further consultation in the family it was advised that she fire the captain and crew, then sell the vessel for what she could get. This was done. Our teacher gave the little girl a good mark for the voyage. In later years this child made a successful career in deluxe ladies' garments.

We youngsters were as interested in violence, train and

bank robberies, and gunfighters as children elsewhere, but we were not fooled about the character of the outlaws. We had a pretty solid feeling that they were cowardly, lazy, and reaped where they had not sown. Only occasionally did lurid incidents occur, as the law had been established on the Western Slope for several decades.

One lovely morning in Delta, some thirty-five miles away, Ray Simpson, a quiet Kentuckian who owned the hardware store, a fantastic marksman, had just finished cleaning his Sharps' rifle. Across the unpaved street A. T. Blackley, cashier and co-founder of the Farmers' and Merchants' Bank, had just opened for business. Blackley was a leading citizen, married to a handsome wife who played the church organ. They had eight children.

At this moment three horsemen rode into the alley behind the bank. They were the McCarty gang. Tom held the horses while Bill and Fred entered the bank where Blackley and his associate Wolbert were working at their desks. Blackley rose to serve them.

"Put up your hands and be damn quiet," Fred said. Blackley replied, "You'll never get away with this." Wolbert reached for his six-shooter. "Throw it on the floor and move 'round here to the cashier's window," commanded Bill McCarty. Blackley shouted loud for help. Fred blew the top of his head off. The bandits gathered up all cash in sight, remounted and moved north on the Grand Junction road.

Ray Simpson had been alerted by the gun shot. He watched places where the men must cross into the open. Shooting from the hip he knocked Bill McCarty dead, from the saddle. A second shot killed Fred, and a third brought down one of the riderless horses. But Tom McCarty got away and was never captured.

Mary Blackley labored hard through many years rearing the eight children by working out, giving music lessons, and taking in washing. For years Ray Simpson received menacing letters from Tom McCarty. Finally to give peace of mind to his family he moved to California without giving anyone a forwarding address.

We enacted many holdups in our games, but we knew the swinish makeup of the desperadoes. There were no Robin Hoods among them.

Any sheriff, deputy, or policeman among us was called the Law. Judges, often untrained in legal procedure were, in general, trusted men of character, common sense, and not seldom with an ironic humor. They handed out rough justice, quickly, without tedious procedures. Stories gathered about picturesque types. We claimed some sort of relationship with an old fellow who has been written up as "The Law West of the Pecos." There were tall yarns about him, but the same episodes were ascribed to many other officers. Judges doubtless copied one another's style.

A yarn goes that this judge rode in one morning to the shack that served as his courtroom. He asked the deputy if there was anything on the docket. "Yes," the deputy replied, "there's a half-breed cattle thief tied up with a lariat to a mesquite tree out yonder." The judge took a fresh chew of tobacco, arranged his papers, and said, "Bring the son-of-a-bitch in and give him a fair trial." This story was accredited to several judges.

Nearly all of us were collectors. There was a relish for Civil War equipment. One kid had a cavalry saddle in good condition. We had bits of uniform, shell and cartridge cases, pistols, rifles, caps, slouch hats, even old boots and overcoats. A sword was a treasure while a usable pair of blue Union Army trousers, with a yellow cavalry or white infantry stripe, gave immense prestige. There was a quiet conspiracy among mothers. If some child were ill, and ordinary tricks were exhausted to persuade quiet and sleep, mothers would take from the closet a well-worn, and sometimes moth-eaten, gray or blue overcoat which had been in the smoke of battle, and lay it over a fretful boy or girl, that settled it!

In addition to Civil War material we had a special relish for anything to do with Indians and weapons. One little girl had several hundred arrowheads, others had tomahawks, stone axes, hunting spears, leather garments and moccasins decorated with colored beads and porcupine quills. Several girls made presentable feathered headdresses. It was a nuisance to our mothers and fathers, but we boys traded bleached deer, cow, and horse skulls which we found on the open range, fastening them up at the ends of barns and sheds. Two old Indians knew sites where good flints were dug in the old days for arrowheads. Indians would heat the flint rocks, then drop water upon them to induce fractures. Further work was done on these chips which were made into arrowheads. Many were crude, but some were beautifully shaped.

Five-cent novels had great vogue among the boys. These must have been published by the million. There were many series, *Pluck and Luck, Old King Brady, Buffalo Bill, Liberty Boys of Seventy-Six,* and the exploits of a Dick Merriwell, a formidable sort of Stover-at-Yale type, only more worthy, and a number of others. One boy kept a storeroom we constructed in the top of his father's barn where everyone in our gang was honor bound to bring all his purchases. If that cache could be found now, collectors would pay a fortune for it.

From these exciting sheets we read not altogether inaccurate accounts of the Little Italys and Chinatowns of great cities, about crime and punishment, heroic deeds on the battlefield, and upon the sea, and the winning of the West. If some aspects were lurid and overdramatized, five-cent novels were never lewd or pornographic. Our parents and teachers frowned on this reading but as I look back on it I can see no harm. At any rate, we would not have been perusing *The Vicar of Wakefield* or *Pride and Prejudice!* These exciting tales did develop a relish for reading which doubtless many transferred to better literature in years ahead.

Winter offers ranchers a chance to catch up on odd jobs such as repair of farm implements and harness. Sets of harness were taken apart, scrubbed and oiled, with new pieces set in where necessary, a job which fell to me. I had a fair set of tools, heavy needles used by saddlers with which one doubled the stitches, thrusting them in from each side; I also had waxed thread, cans of oil, spare snaps and buckles and saddle soap for bridles, reins, and saddles. It was quite a long job, done in the cellar by lantern light on Saturdays, with pleasant smells not only of harness but also of fruit and vegetables stored away in sacks and boxes.

There were many tasks for Saturday. One chore was churning butter, which I much disliked. At times when we had a lot of cream from several cows, a wooden churn with a dasher was used which agitated the cream and eventually caused a separation of butterfat from the whey. When there was only a small amount of cream, or a quick need developed in our kitchen, I employed a half-gallon Mason jar, simply rocking it back and forth in my arms for some twenty minutes. In both cases as soon as the butterfat clotted, the liquid was drained off as buttermilk. The remaining fat was kneaded with a broad wooden paddle until all liquid was forced out. Then salt was worked into the lump and the job was done. Cows feeding in sagebrush country often ate wild onions which highly flavored all milk and butter.

Another job was sorting potatoes and apples. Before frost we stored against the winter about thirty bushels of apples, many pumpkins, an ample supply of potatoes, and several boxes of onions. Along the walls on rough shelves were hundreds of quarts of peaches, cherries, plums, applesauce, apple and peach butter, jellies, and preserves. Also there was a barrel of dill pickles and one of sauerkraut.

Potatoes were the most trouble. They tended to sprout quite rapidly after storing, the sprouts taking away the good quality. It was not a hard job to pull away or brush off the sprouts, but it was cold in the cellar and hands became quickly crusted with dirt. Rotten potatoes have one of the most disgusting smells. Sorting apples was easy, all one needed to do was to throw aside the ones with specks.

Hubbard squash is a fine vegetable. We always stored dozens of them against the winter. They are easy to raise and are a nutritious food when baked. Sweet potatoes do not grow easily on irrigated land. They tend to burn or blight. The Hubbard squash is an adequate substitute in every way, splendid either when baked or in pie.

Hunting was good, but the day of professional hunters and trappers was about gone. A few men conducted Easterners into the high mountains on trips, but were careful never to take them to the best grouse, deer, and bear country! One day my father and I were on an excursion in the hills for the fun of it. We were near a big blackberry patch on the Big Muddy. We saw high bushes moving, and there in front of us was a handsome grizzly bear. There are not many left. We watched him for a half hour. After eating his fill, he shambled off without paying much attention to us.

In addition to the abundance of cottontails there were numbers of weasels, a few mink, and always coyotes on our ranch. Only once did I see a mountain lion, or cougar, a very solitary and elusive beast about half the size of lions in a circus, lithe, tawny and beautiful. He walked along a sandstone ledge, turned his head in contempt, gave a silent spit, and disappeared in the bushes.

The whole Rocky Mountain region in former days had been a harvest ground for a tough lot of trappers known as the Mountain Men. Their period lasted little more than a generation; only a few of these rugged types were still alive in the Gunnison River country. Beaver pelts had been used in making felt hats in earlier years. Trappers lived a hard life, many taking Indian women as mates. Their day passed as markets and styles changed.

In some localities beavers were nearly exterminated. Near us the beaver population was coming back. In many small, high valleys there was one beaver dam after another. These clever animals especially liked a stream bordered by aspens and willows from which they made not only dams but also a central lodge with underwater openings where trees and branches were buried for winter food. Seldom was a beaver any longer killed in our valley.

We children learned much from burros. Like horses they were unknown in the Americas until Spaniards brought them. Our burros differ markedly from the trim, short-haired, fine-boned donkeys of Ireland, Italy, and other European lands. The typical Western burro has bigger bones and hoofs and stands a hand taller. In winter his hair is a veritable fur, shaggy and thick. Mostly they were whitish-gray in color. As descendants of packtrain animals which had been turned loose, or had escaped, there was a scattering of them up through the Rocky Mountains as far as Canada. Many were owned by settlers; some lived and bore their young, who looked like comic jackrabbits, on the same ranches for generations. Far more ran loose on Government reserves, which consisted of almost all the mountains proper. Burros were gentle and approachable. Often when a rancher wanted a few for a pack trip in the hills, or one for a child, he would go out, make his choice, and bring the burro in. It was a custom among us to let burros without a home feed with the ranch stock in winter months. Burros were light eaters, existing on almost anything.

There are legends about the donkey, or burro, since the time of Balaam's ass. They have the finest eyes in the world, clear and beautiful, with the patience and sorrows of God in them. Devout Indians and Mexicans have a theory that burros have a spiritual significance. They refer to the cross in darker color which many bear—the black streak along the back from mane to tail, traversed by another stripe on the withers running down the legs. All of us children loved burros; their unmusical braying was a friendly call out in the waste.

The care of horses' hoofs is always important especially in winter. A good part of this work fell on me. We had a fair blacksmith shop on the ranch, especially tools and materials for horseshoeing, and the sharpening of axes and plowshares. In autumn we pulled shoes off all horses which we were not working. Hoofs keep growing like fingernails so that a shoe left on too long causes damage to a hoof, as it binds too tightly. It matters little if an unshod horse slips around a bit. With draft or saddle horses to be used on roads or about the ranch it is a far different matter. These working horses we sharpshod for winter by hammering out the calks to a thin edge. The two rear calks on a shoe would be turned in different directions to prevent slipping. A horse well sharpshod can even be raced on icy roads or frozen lakes.

However, two dangers had to be avoided with sharpshod horses. Some animals interfere, as do humans; that is, one leg hits against the other, which can cause cruel cuts. The second danger is that some horses are habitual kickers. Without shoes they generally do little harm to one another, but a sharpshod horse can do much damage. Kickers we placed in a separate corral in the winter. In the cavalry it was generally the custom to tie a small knot of white ribbon or twine on the tail of a kicker to warn of danger. More than in regions of abundant rainfall it was necessary to oil hoofs to prevent cracking. Wide hoofs of Clydesdales was one reason they were never as favored in the arid West as some other breeds.

We had one filly named Mulette who was a delight, and a nuisance. She was not a blooded beastie, but she had spirit. We would leave her outside the feeding corrals for weeks at a time to prevent her bedeviling older horses. When some tired old mare dozed near the fence of heavy cedar logs, Mulette would sneak up, turn her head sidewise, thrust it through the logs, giving the mare a sharp bite, then run off in apparent delight.

Mulette despised pigs but liked to torment them. On hot days shoats and sows took to the shade by their log fence, covered with mud, grunting gently, minding their own business. Mulette would approach quietly, grab one and bite until her teeth popped when she let go. The victim would scream, taking off like a torpedo across the pigpen.

She had another unseemly trick. In the midst of the cow

corral was a snubbing post used for wrapping a rope around when were were working over animals. This was sawed off square, at the height of a man's head. In good weather we would milk in the open air, often placing a bucket on top of the snubbing post. Mulette, when allowed in the cow corral, would, on occasion, run by the post, jump high, and with one hoof knock off the bucket. She was eventually banned.

We were never bothered much with snakes but in some sections near us rattlers were a pest. Many cowboys and local buckaroos carried a four-foot pole with a piece of chain on the end for a flail. When they encountered a rattler they could, on foot or horseback, more easily dispatch him than with a gun, for snakes are hard to hit with a bullet. With a shotgun it is different, but few men carried a shotgun on a horse. We kids collected rattles. Pigs soon rid a ranch of rattlers. Although pigs seem slow and lazy, they can move like lightning when they wish to do so.

Evenings were long in winters with no possibility of outside amusements. My stepmother possessed a beautiful voice, and, fortunately for many of us, enjoyed reading aloud. Men working on the ranch came in to the large kitchen with a basket of apples and winter pears upon the table and settled down for the reading. Grimes Golden, Jonathan, Northern Spy, Spitzenburg, Winesap, Rome Beauty, and Missouri Pippins were eaten as my stepmother read from such books the *The Tale of Two Cities, The Prince of India, Ben Hur, Les Miserables, The Wandering Jew,* and popular novels of the day, such as *The Crossing, The Crisis, Dri and I, The Clansman, The Leopard's Spots, The Right of Way, That Printer of Udells* and other books by Rex Beach, Marion Crawford, Edith Wharton, and Harold Bell Wright. These evenings were a boon to men after a hard day's work as snow settled feet thick over the silent, gloomy mountains. Years later, I read of the death of Opie Read. We had at least twenty of his books, *The Starbucks, The Waters of Caney Fork, The Jucklins, Old Ebenezer* and others. He was the famous author of *The Arkansaw*

Traveller. Father read largely Dumas, Dickens, Thackeray and modern writers, especially those with a sociological bent, as well as current mining literature. He was now a rancher, but the mines were dear to him.

We took many magazines. As there were no playmates about I had plenty of time to read. Theodore Roosevelt was in the White House busting trusts and enjoying himself generally. I recall reading a long series of articles by Ray Stannard Baker and Ida M. Tarbell on great corporations, and Thomas W. Lawson's diatribes in *Everybody's* on "Frenzied Finance." The Beef Trust had recently been declared illegal by the Supreme Court. The canal across the Isthmus of Panama was becoming a nearer possibility. I followed every step of the negotiations until the great ditch was finished, Colonel Goethals and General Gorgas becoming my earliest heroes. There were exciting articles about investigation of the Equitable Life Assurance Society. For the first time the Federal Government was trying in earnest to check rough-and-tumble methods of high finance. The Lewis and Clark Centennial at Portland, Oregon, started me reading on that section of the West. I found a stack of old illustrated papers in the smokehouse containing pictures and articles on the Russo-Japanese War and of the peace proceedings at Portsmouth, New Hampshire. The most exciting pictures I cut out to paste on the inside walls of the woodshed and the privie.

Sometimes the men would ask Father political and economic questions. President Roosevelt had just advocated an inheritance tax. Father was for it and also for an income tax, both considered wildly subversive by conservatives.

In the spring of 1906 came news of the San Francisco earthquake. All the ranchers contributed to a boxcar of food, which, with hundreds of other cars, was sent West to the Golden Gate. We learned later that two of our relatives were killed in the disaster. General Pershing's wife had also perished.

During this time there were frequent interventions by

our Army, Navy and State Department in the affairs of Santo Domingo, Cuba, and the nations bordering the Carribean. The Standard Oil Company was indicted for receiving rebates. Such miscellaneous events employed my mind as I tried to piece together a picture of the world and its conflicting interests.

When we had finished with our magazines they went up and down the valley from ranch to ranch. Men sometimes rode ten, even fifteen miles, to take a bundle home for a month's reading. Anyone passing always stopped to exchange news. There was no telephone so we welcomed these brief visits.

Most of our people in the North Fork Valley were of old American stock with a few settlers of newer vintage. Railway section hands on some divisions were entirely Greek. On others they were all Mexican—but no mixtures. The few Germans who had arrived in the early days were among the most careful ranchers in the valley. There was a German Mesa a few miles distant where a number lived. Once we had a deserter from the German army work for us for over a year. He would never meet or talk with our German neighbors. He was not ashamed of his desertion, but probably would have been embarrassed anyway. He had served in the Far East and in East and South West Africa. We boys dragged many stories out of him. The majority of ranchers were descendants of people who, over a few generations, had worked their way West from the eastern seaboard.

Men from Cornwall were almost all hard-rock miners, but now and then one would give up the mines to try ranching. They were always known as Cousin Jacks and were famous for their choral singing.

We children had an unflagging interest in animals about us. Throughout most of the arid West one finds prairie dogs. They tend to make settlements we called prairie dog towns. Some of the towns must have been inhabited for centuries for, over an area of an acre or more, burrowings carried above ground raised the level of the town a foot or more above the surrounding land. Prairie dogs were amusing and clever creatures. We observed, and naturalists have confirmed, that rabbits, snakes and owls occupied the same underground tunnels in amity. Prairie dogs are voracious eaters; near one of their towns alfalfa would be eaten off, leaving large barren patches.

It was quite a job to clear a ranch of prairie dogs. When water was turned into a prairie dog town from an irrigation ditch it might take hours to flood all the galleries. Later the water would soak gradually to the surface and evaporate, leaving alkaline salts, a crust which killed vegetation. It sometimes took years to reclaim a prairie dog town to fruitful cultivation.

We boys were not natural killers, but prairie dogs were a pest, therefore they provided legitimate targets. Each of us had a Marlin or a Winchester .22 caliber repeater. A few boys used their fathers' Krags, and .45-70s, but ammunition for these was too expensive for most of us. We improved our marksmanship on the prairie dogs.

Some boys became crack shots practicing on these rodents. Years later I qualified as a sharpshooter in the Infantry, although I was not as good as some of my friends in the North Fork. There was an abundance of cottontail rabbits about in the sage, no jackrabbits, as later in Idaho. Sometimes I would take my Marlin repeater and get two cottontails before going to school. They were delicious eating. And, we were hard up!

Fuel is always important, especially so on a farm or ranch. In Kansas and the Indian Territory, we relied, basically, on corncobs. In Colorado we had great riches in fuel for there was a Farmers' Coal Bank where in winter a crew dug out soft coal of an excellent quality. Members of the organization, if they would do the hauling themselves, could buy coal for a dollar and a quarter a ton.

Then, too, below the belt of fir and pine which stopped at timberline there were thousands of scrub cedars. Some of these twenty-foot trees were perhaps a thousand years old. They made any sort of fire one could wish, with a most pleasing aromatic smell.

There were grave accidents at times among our neighbors, not from automobiles, for there were none. But now and then a man would suffer frostbite, or a bad fall from a horse. There were accidents from runaways, and mishaps in the mines. One close friend, a splendid horseman, was inspecting his cows on their summer pasturage high up on the Government Reserve near Mount Gunnison when he was struck by lightning. His body was strapped upon a packhorse to be carried to his home; our whole valley was saddened.

We had no near neighbors, but good ones some distance away. One of these was Aaron Clough, an elderly Oregon Trail Scout. No one knew how old Aaron Clough was, certainly not he. He had a splendid ranch, a good water right, had prospered, but lived in as primitive a manner as he would have done in 1850. He had fine stock, magnificent alfalfa fields and a large one-room cabin made of cottonwood logs. The roof was also made of logs, with sod laid on top, then a thick covering of adobe. On this grew various grasses and wild flowers. His cabin was warm in winter, cool in summer, and the roof never leaked unless a ground squirrel made a tunnel or a house in it. Clough knew all the prominent pioneers of the Rockies and the Northwest, real and phony; he also knew the difference. He had fought hostile Indians and renegade white men. Once he made the trip to the mouth of the Columbia River by way of Wyoming, Montana, and the Yellowstone country in the dead of winter, nearly starving until rescued by a friendly tribe. He spoke several Indian tongues.

Aaron Clough looked like an Old Testament prophet, long hair and beard, friendly, with piercing gray eyes, a great Adam's apple which went up and down when he talked, a bass voice, loud, but melodious, and gracious manners—a natural gentleman. We children were always welcome in his spotless cabin as he never minded our demands for stories of his adventures. He cooked and washed for himself. On any visit we were welcome to homemade bread and butter and a big helping from the pot of pork and beans which was always on his stove. If he had lived in the Middle Ages he would have been, on his own prowess, a duke or a baron.

Old-timers had the best stories for the children. Doubtless tales were embroidered but we learned much. Many had been in the Indian wars, nearly all had hunted buffalo when these great beasts roamed the plains in millions. In the olden days there were immense flocks of prairie chickens, now extinct through stupid, careless killing. Two of our old neighbors had crossed the Isthmus of Panama in the California Gold Rush days. One had fought in a posse against the Dalton Gang. Several had ventured into the Yellowstone, and the Glacier Lake country in Montana, and beyond up into Canada in days when there was no organized government in those parts.

Two queer old fellows were water witches. They took hazel branches, grasped them by the two forks and walked slowly over a place where someone wanted to dig a well. One of these men was a faker, but the other seemed to possess an obscure power which caused the stick to point down when a place was traversed where there was good underground water.

There was also a beeman who had a way with him. He would put sugar in his hand and then follow bees to their cache in hollow trees and cliffs. We boys accompanied him at a safe distance. Often in summer we saw him hiving a swarm on his place, with bees by the thousands on his head and face and beard. He came to a tragic end. A dog started barking at one swarm he was working. The bees became excited and stung the old man to death.

Not too far away lived an old-timer who had made the Cherokee Run. He was a tall, thin man dying of consumption. He had slept on the Kansas-Oklahoma line the night of April 21-22, 1889. With a hundred thousand others on horseback, on foot, and in every form of buckboard, carriage and wagon he had raced for land on the Cherokee

Strip, one of the most astonishing methods any nation ever conceived to open a rich new region to settlement. He had ridden one horse until it fell in a gopher hole. He shot him, saddled a second he was leading, and gained the piece of his choice. Hard times and ill health drove him out and another had his cabin, his fields and well, and all his improvements.

There were on some of the ranches old, weathered prairie schooners which had been used in that crazy race of '89. A few people were interested in preserving them, but not many. On some were still discernable old slogans, "In God we Trust; In Kansas we Busted." On others were "Damn Kansas," and on one "White Capped In Indiana." Our old friend told us that in the run carts and wagons were drawn by one mule and a cow, a yoke of oxen, a burro and a horse, and all possible combinations of animals. Some men started out with wheelbarrows. One woman I knew had made the dash with a baby carriage and had later driven off two men with a Winchester when they tried to squat on her land.

On the Cherokee Run the Government, at President Benjamin Harrison's order, had stopped all trains leading into the area of 10,000 square miles for two weeks. The whole region was surrounded by U.S. Cavalry and no white man was allowed to enter. At eleven thirty on the morning of April 22, the commanding officer of the cavalry stood watch in hand. When the hour of noon came a bugler sounded a few notes. This was followed by the firing of army carbines which ran around the vast circle of the "Strip." The race was on! The line ran roughly from the Cherokee outlet near the Kansas line to the South Canadian River near Purcell, thence to the Santa Fe Railroad Lines. The old consumptive reported that there was so much excitement that he knew hundreds of people who swore that no guns had been fired at all when the race started. Several died of heart attacks; a baby was born in a wagon which was going at full gallop across blue-stem prairie.

On the day of the run five Santa Fe trains rolled slowly

from the north and five from the south not to exceed the speed of horses. Settlers were allowed to go on these trains if they wished to do so. There were not a few sooners, people who had slipped through cavalry lines and had already staked out fertile quarter sections of land. Some of these sooners were shot by irate settlers who had made the run legitimately, some were evicted by the cavalry, most stayed where they were.

At one time my dying consumptive friend had been in an Apache war against Geronimo. I often saw that famous chief in his extreme old age, hard-eyed, grizzled, wrinkled, and evil looking, a killer whose anger never died away. Who could blame Indians for fighting back against the whites? There had been atrocities on both sides, but, as far as I know, there never has been a treaty until very recent times which the United States made with the Indians that was ever intended to be kept.

One old character we called Uncle Job, although he was no blood relation, was friendly with all us children. In those days a farmer shipping four carloads or more of cattle or pigs to the great packinghouses in Omaha, Kansas City, St. Louis, or Chicago was entitled to a free pass in the caboose. Uncle Job had such a pass to Omaha. Aunt Clara pressed his best suit, cleaned his ten-gallon hat, provided a big clothes basket of delicious food and saw him off with many warnings regarding behavior in the big city. In Omaha, Uncle Job successfully disposed of his stock, and, as he had to wait overnight to catch a freight train back, he decided to go to a theater, which he had never before done. He was comfortably seated in the front row still wearing his big hat as he always did at home, when the curtain went up. A vaudeville team put on an Apache dance. The man did a lot of acrobatic turns and commenced to knock his female partner about the stage in assumed ferocity.

Uncle Job, unused to such things, took all seriously. He endured the seeming cruelty for a time, then rose, shaking his cane at the actor.

"Young man, stop abusing that lady," he cried out above the orchestra.

The audience thought it was part of the show and loved it.

The actor was somewhat disconcerted, but after looking at Uncle Job continued his routine. The old man, after a few minutes sprang to his feet again, climbed up on the stage, grabbed the dancer amidship and threw him over into the front row where he landed on an old couple nearly breaking them in two. Uncle Job then stomped out of the theater with loud curses upon such an immoral performance. The audience howled. Aunt Clara never let Job make such trips alone after that journey.

The wisdom of these older men and women was respected, their advice generally followed. One couple had raised a large family near us. The husband was much older than the wife, who still had romantic inclinations, carrying on an affair with a United States Marshal in a neighboring district. All the countryside knew about this. Uncle Job was consulted. He listened carefully to the husband's tale then requested him to come back next morning for an answer. The language of oil fields which were being opened up had crept into our daily speech. In the morning, when the offended man appeared, Uncle Job said, "Sam, I have given this matter a whole night's thought. I love you both. Martha has been a wonderful wife and mother. It would not be right to let this break up your home. She has something to say for herself. You could never have done as well through these years with anyone else. Here's what I believe: it's better to have a half interest in a gusher than a dry hole outright." The husband thought for long minutes. "I guess you're right, Job," he said. In a few months the Marshal was moved, and all was well.

There was one close family friend we called Aunt Margaret, although no relation. She had the body of an Aphrodite, tall and perfectly proportioned. Margaret was full of wisdom. In a discussion, when a number of women were canning peaches one day, she uttered her judgment on the way the world wags. Said Aunt Margaret, "Aside from carnal enjoyments, and the main consolations of religion, there is no fun in the world like spending other peoples' money."

From time to time some unmarried girl would become pregnant. To such a one she would say, "If you don't want the peaches, don't shake the trees!" But she always defended these girls. Most young women, married or unmarried, in our neighborhood consulted with Aunt Margaret about the facts of life, marriage, husbands, and children.

During one big blizzard Aunt Margaret burst into our kitchen. She was holding her breasts, quite plainly in distress.

"Come in, come in," said my stepmother. "Where have you been so long. We have missed you like a front tooth!"

"Gawd Amighty! I've frozen me nipples," Margaret shouted. She immediately stripped off her blouse and undershirt. My stepmother rubbed snow on her breasts. I was bundled up and sent forth to the stable for remedies, where as junior veterinary to our animals I had a cache of Sloane's Liniment, various spavin cures, De Witts Witch Hazel salve for cuts and saddle sores, and a number of simple nostrums.

First I slapped on a lot of Sloane's Liniment, which with us was a cure-all for almost anything. It burned Aunt Margaret, and a lot of it ran down to her middle. She hollered like a good fellow. My stepmother took a pan of cream, scooped up a handful and rubbed it on her. This emollient after a time soothed Margaret's pain. She sat for an hour drinking coffee, discussing local news and the big storm. Then she dressed and took off for her home two miles away in the smothering whiteness of the blizzard.

Next spring when we had a family gathering, Margaret came along. At noon she was asked how her frostbites turned out. She took off her blouse and went round the circle. She had nursed six sons, and her breasts had been a bit chewed up, but now they were round and pink. They had peeled off and returned to the same beauty she had had as a young woman.

All of us boys learned to smoke—coffee, dried catalpa beans, cubebs, buggywhip rattan, and finally tobacco. No one who has never experienced tobacco sickness can realize what some boys suffer in learning to smoke.

There were almost no tailor-made cigarettes in those days. The first I can recall were Sweet Caporals. We would persuade some older boy to buy Duke's Mixture, a mild cigarette tobacco, at five cents for a good-sized pack. Those who had more money to spend would pay ten cents for a smaller pack of Bull Durham. Every store gave away small packets of cigarette papers with advertisements printed on the cover in much the same fashion as paper matches are distributed now.

Chewing tobacco was in vogue. Granger's Twist, Star, and Horseshoe were the most favored plug tobaccos. There was also very sweet Piper Heidsick, heavily laden with licorice. Among others there was Drummonds Natural Leaf. Most chewing tobacco had tin tags pressed into the surface which were lifted off to exchange for various articles listed in catalogues, like Green Stamps are today. We collected tin stars, horseshoes and other emblems from older friends. There was a heavy traffic in these among the children for they were exchangeable for fishing gear, gloves, even air rifles. Every parent forbade the use of tobacco; every boy used it when he could.

No sex education was given in school or home, but as I look back on it we were not badly shortchanged. We all had animals in our homes, saw beasts of the field mate and bear their young, and we were aware of courting and love-making by creatures of the wild. We knew scandals among married people, and we were quite aware when women members of our families were expecting babies, and how they came by them. There was no period of excessive interest or severe strain for most of us.

On every ranch there were numerous dogs and cats. The dogs were nearly all of a type we called shepherds, not purebred, but of all fancy dogs I have since met, none compared in behavior, intelligence, and affection with our mongrels. Cats were not only useful to keep down mice and other rodents, but serviceable also as friends and pets. I had two enormous yellow toms named Thomas W. Lawson and Theodore Roosevelt. They were characters who preferred warm nests outdoors to living in the house. There was always plentiful food for them from the kitchen. They were friendly with the dogs, cows, and horses. The chimney of the ranch house was an iron tube which gave off a certain amount of heat as it emerged through the roof of the shed kitchen. In winter the cats used to sit with backs to the warm chimney surveying the goings-on around the ranch.

Inasmuch as there was no organized recreation or entertainment, we had something better—enjoying the tricks, antics, squabbles, and play of both domestic and wild animals and birds on the ranch.

Some birds and small animals seem to prefer being near people's homes. Robins are especially gentle. They are very amusing as they make their six or seven stifflegged hops turning their heads to listen for worms, and, having seized one, bracing their feet, leaning backward, until either they pull it out or are chased away by another bird eager for a tidbit. No other birds with us seemed to like living so close to homesteads. The ubiquitous field sparrows were great eaters and had a comic way of scratching with both feet at once!

A few boys in town kept pigeons. Some had fancy ones, fantails and tumblers. One had several homing pigeons which he released at long distances from his loft. They quickly and invariably made their way home, but very few ranch boys had pigeons.

At the time my father built the irrigation system and bought his thirteen ranches we only had access by stagecoach some forty miles over unpaved roads to the narrow-gauge Denver and Rio Grande rail line at Delta. Somewhere around 1900 the D&RG extended its narrow-gauge line up the North Fork of the Gunnison as far as Somerset, where a big coal mine was opened. A trainload of coal was taken out daily. This all had to be reloaded into broad-gauge cars at Grand Junction. The same thing happened with the over one thousand refrigerator cars of fruit which went out of our valley each autumn. Some years later the railway brought in hundreds of section hands from other divisions to lay the wide gauge over the whole length of our spur line in one long day.

The principal occupation of the North Fork had shifted from cattle until it was predominantly a fruit-growing community, a change which had taken place in many valleys in the irrigated West. The fruit business became a hysteria. Values rose until a few highly developed orchards sold for as high as a thousand dollars an acre. The valley, as so many high, irrigated Western valleys, produced good fruit but there were always heavy expenses to be met. Some men made money but a large number failed. It took from five to eight years for the trees to bear after they were planted and there were taxes and water rent, pruning, and various kinds of sprays when the trees did start yielding in marketable quantities. If there was a good crop there generally was a poor market and between local costs, pests, frost, hail, freight rates and commissions, hundreds lost savings of a lifetime and borrowed more to sink in the same hopeless enterprise.

Around the fringe of the fruit-raising valleys old cattlemen stayed by their cows and alfalfa, reaping smaller profits but more regular ones. Their methods were radically changed as years went by, but many of them made small fortunes and held on to them.

During harvest days everyone worked at white heat. Gathering a peach crop is almost a matter of hours. Even the minister dismissed church early, going back to his ranch with wife and children to pick peaches. Packinghouses worked day and night. High officials of the Denver and Rio Grande Railroad came in person to superintend the distribution of hundreds of yellow refrigerator cars. For a few weeks the valley was like a town when gold or oil is struck. Migratory labor poured in by the hundreds, some honest and hard working, along with hoodlums of the worst order.

Migrant labor, a necessity in the United States to harvest seasonal crops from Florida to Washington, was in those days in no locality adequately housed. In this period the I.W.W. sprang up to protect these men against rapacious employers and crooked constables, and often became rapacious in its turn. The "Grapes of Wrath" is an old crop in the West. Both sides abused their powers and have a long and bitter history to live down. Intervening years have seen no solution of the problem of seasonal, migratory laborers. We could not have gathered our fruit without them. Mexican *braceros,* even when entering illegally, have brought benefits not only to the workers, but to American farmers as well.

There was a small bearing orchard on the Minnesota Creek ranch. We harvested on an average about two thousand dollars' worth of fruit per year from this. It was our main salable crop, so, in all, it was rather slim pickings. All of us boys acquired a fair amount of information about the fruit business. In summer or winter, with or without fruit or leaves, I could identify over fifty varieties of apple trees, but was not so skillful about pears and peaches. Although I gave myself fully to the work in hand I never cared too much about raising fruit. There were too many hazards and circumstances over which one had no control. If I had been given a choice I would far rather have been on a cattle ranch in the mountains, with Aaron Clough, but not in an outfit with feeding pens on the great plains.

The Fourth of July was the one holiday of the year in our little mountain community. There were bucking contests, drilling exhibitions by teams of the Modern Woodmen and Woodmen of the World, churning, sewing, cooking and canning exhibitions, with prizes. Children were allowed riding contests with burros. One boy had a burro which was notoriously hard to ride. The little animal just fit under a pole hitching rack at the side of the street. After trying vainly to dislocate his rider, he would bolt for the rack, dragging off the young bronco buster! Every boy saved his money for the Fourth. There would be chances to treat a girl to ice cream, or, maybe to go to a ball game between local braves and some nearby town. There were no movies in those days in our valley.

Another big event was horse races on a level road by the river. Ten riders started a half mile up the lane. About one hundred yards from the finish was a bridge across a deep creek, only wide enough to accommodate four animals abreast. What would have happened had all ten taken the bridge together we never experienced, for, as in all derbys, horses soon trailed one another, and all always passed the hazard safely.

One man who often worked for us on the main ranch, and for a long period was our foreman, had a profound influence upon me. He was not a wisecracker, or a talkative local comedian, of which there is always one in every country district, although he had plenty of wit. Rather, he was a natural philosopher of singular intellectual gifts. Perhaps the human race has had others equal to Plato, Socrates, Galileo, or Dante, lighted minds, whom the accidents of history left unrevealed—some noble peasant thinker in Siberia or unlettered and unknown philosopher on our Great Plains, or in jungles or fastnesses of other continents.

Don Meek had ridden the rods, hobo fashion, over the United States, had been a cowpoke, ranch hand, miner, and hunter. He was at home with a blanket, frying pan and coffee bucket under the stars, never arrogant with inferiors, unabashed with those who had formal learning. He was brave without ferocity and strong without violence.

He was something of an engineer, clever at building roads, erecting cabins, irrigation ditches, houses and barns, and a good orchardist. There was nothing he could not do with cows and horses. He broke, branded and gentled wild range horses, castrated and shod them, and treated the sick. We had a blacksmith shop on the place, where he did good iron work. In rough wrestling and other games he was equal to any in the valley, and he was a crack shot.

When Don strode stiff legged across the corral we all knew he was the best among us. Of medium height, black from the sun, level gray eyes, thick hair, straight nose, strong, even white teeth, erect as a soldier, with legs slightly bowed by the saddle, he was impressive. His rakish Stetson was worn a little to one side, his much used cattlemen's boots were always clean, fitted with long shank spurs with enormous rowels he seldom employed. Don wore thick leather chaps, stained with cooking grease and the blood of stock and wild animals, scarred by thorny brush. He never used fancy kerchiefs, loud shirts, or bear or sheepskin chaps. He was no show-off, dressing in the best, but also the simplest clothing for the job in hand.

Sharp lines about his eyes, common to those living in dry lands, gave a squint, not unbecoming in his weathered face. When conversing he wore a faint smile, not exactly ironic, but tolerant without condescension. He could be astringent but was never cynical.

Don was no saint, or did he pretend to be. He liked good whiskey, carried it well, enjoyed drinking with friends, but he never became silly, pugnacious, or a nuisance. He was a good dancer and singer, knowing a lot of cowboy songs that he loved to teach us youngsters.

Although Don was almost unschooled, he was a keen reader, and, above all, an original thinker and a creative listener. Out on the range, or on the ranch, in long Socratic dialogues he delved beneath surface appearances of life and of things, laying before us for such consideration as our lesser minds could give, major enigmas of ethics, science, religion, politics, the problem of knowledge, and the problems of evil and of good.

Often, by campfires in the high country, when the day's work was done, he would roll homemade cigarettes and respond to our queries. Under his leading we would review our prejudices, correct or amplify our premises. In anthropology, or sociology, in other contexts, he could have been a Sumner, in philosophy, a Whitehead. Without any of the terminology of classical philosophy Don was discussing, on his own, knotty questions of epistomology, logic, ethics, and theology which had tormented the minds of Berkeley, Spinoza, Descartes, Schopenhauer, Bergson and the others.

We youngsters would question and listen as constellations rose over spruce-covered ridges to the east and rotated toward the zenith as the Milky Way streamed across the night.

When sex was discussed Don was explicit, always avoiding anything prurient. When queried on religion he was rather vague, but we nevertheless felt he had a tremendous reverence toward a certain hierarchy of values. He held land, bread, drink, animals, and men sacred, and seemed a pantheist. Accumulated knowledge and native intelligence he cherished, but he treasured above all else a wonder and respect for all life. He would pick up a pine cone from the saddle and discuss it for long miles, its structure, the number of seeds it contained, their possibility of germinating and taking root, the length of time the spruce had been on earth and its chance, as a species, to survive.

One cold winter night, with the temperature some thirty degrees below zero, we rode together from his ranch on top of Black Canyon about forty miles to my father's place. Neither of our horses was sharpshod. We slipped and floundered over the roads, dismounting every hour to walk a mile or so to keep our feet from freezing. We laughed and talked, watching star groups, which seemed very close in the crystalline air as they descended below Black Mesa towering to the west. Finally, we arrived as first light was breaking on Mount Lamborn. We ate a whole chocolate cake, six eggs apiece, with lots of bacon, coffee, and toast. After thawing out he immediately set out for his home.

Don was unconscious of any method or pattern in his questions and reflections. No fixed positions were defended, no axes ground. He listened to the dumbest of us with a comforting respect. As he ruminated, a queer, almost sad, smile brought out fan-shaped wrinkles around his eyes, softening his weather-blackened face. He led us to think on what was substance and what shadow, what was appearance and what reality. Perhaps he had a secret sorrow, a pain borne by men of wisdom, because they know the almost impossible task of handing on distilled experience of one generation to another. He never confessed this, but, at times, when his face was in repose, I felt in a dim way he was heavily burdened with the tragic sense of life.

Out of abstract propositions, seeking some clarifying principle, he would often analyze actions of the county commissioners or other governmental bodies, trying, with fairness, to discover why they behaved as they did regarding roads, schools, water rights, and homestead claims, to discover their motivation, to scrutinize what was done, and to discover what ought to be done.

He never pressed us beyond our ability to absorb, never embarrassed us with superior knowledge, causing a stoppage of thought, when we were unable to contribute in discussing or to articulate our views. Don knew when to let up, to ease off mental tension, just as he would slacken a lariat to give a roped animal time to adjust, space to turn in to prevent injury or panic. He left a private space around our minds and souls. Don was significant to us.

After I left Colorado he moved to a remote region on top of Black Canyon above Sapanero and there established a cattle ranch. He had married a beautiful and gifted woman, daughter of an English clergyman. They reared two splendid sons and enlarged their holdings.

We worked long hours on our ranch, as did our neighbors. We arose before daylight summer and winter. My job was to feed horses, cows, and pigs, to clean stables and do the milking. In season Father and I worked in the orchard, spraying, irrigating, or thinning apples. We cleared new land, picked rock near the mountain, cut wood, and twice each summer mowed and stacked the alfalfa. Hard, unceasing work had made me able to keep up with the men. There was always ten hours' labor in the field, and chores night and morning. An ambition shared by all of us boys was to be known as a good shot, a good worker, and a good horseman.

And there were tensions for my stepmother and I grew to hate each other in those years. She was a person of good taste, clarity of mind, and she had an excellent head for figures. Silently month after month we detested each other. This atmosphere of quiet hatred penetrated our whole life. My father knew it but was helpless to improve matters. Month after month, year after year, the spiritual duel went on coloring much of our thought and way of life. We arose with it in the morning and went to bed with it at night, in bondage to the soil, and to one another.

Books were available at the small library at the Paonia high school and I turned eagerly to the world of the printed page. Father had about the house some volumes on ancient history and the Middle Ages. I found an exercise book, writing out for my pleasure sketches on the life of Ramases II, Tiglath-pileser I, II, and III, Sargon, Sennacherib, Sardanapalus, Nebuchadnezzar, David, Cyrus, Cambyses II, Croesus, Darius, and others. These sketches could not compare favorably with later works by George Trevelyan or Arnold Toynbee!

The zeal for self-improvement which has been the stock-in-trade of writers who have looked with amusement and often contempt upon such efforts among us as Babbitts and Main Streeters, was strong in our country districts. All national magazines carried advertisements of sets of books and individual volumes which could, if properly used, give valuable instruction. For several years I cut out from magazines every ad about Ridpath's *History of the World*, but I was never able to lay hands on enough money to send for it.

This rather lonely period gave me a fondness for animals, especially burros, horses, dogs, and cats. I have as clear memories of many of them, and they have as firm a place in my affection, as any of the people I knew in those years. The interplay of character and temperament among animals and their attitudes to humankind have been a constant source of interest. Can one not appraise individuals and nations by their treatment of animals? Why do so many intelligent and non-sentimental people have a strong affection for them? For one reason, animals are in a state of innocence; they never—as do men—premeditate evil!

And there is something else about the affection between people and animals. Down at the bottom of human hearts and minds are a fair amount of loneliness and a desire, unspoken generally, for relatedness and acceptance. Even in the best ranch families there are gaps; not every boy or girl receives equal affection and attention, or enough to fulfill his or her needs. Even the wisest and best intentioned parents cannot do a perfect job. Among us ranch kids these gaps, slights, omissions, or even prejudices against us, were compensated by mutual friendship and affection with animals. We were related, and we were accepted, thus in the totality of our lives we were not cheated.

Every week or two it was necessary to go to town for groceries. It was three and a half miles to the village to which I carried an empty flour sack for lugging back the purchases. On these trips I always borrowed a few books at the high school library. The long walk to school in term time, morning and evening chores, and a full day's work on Saturdays and often Sundays, left little time, but I learned to read in snatches. It was excellent training for later years.

There was not a great deal of heavy drinking in the North Fork country although there were several well patronized saloons. We had for a time a wonderful fellow as foreman who felt it his duty to get tight every so often and to gallop out of town with two guns blazing. Once, feeling he had overdone his act a bit, he hid out with his horse, back of the ranch, against the mountain lest the deputy sheriff come with a warrant. I carried meals to him and hay for his horse. Nothing happened as a rather tolerant attitude was taken about such antics, as long as no blood was shed. A comfortable habit prevailed whereby when a rancher paid his store debts, a deal was concluded for hay, fruit, horses, or cattle, and the participants would celebrate their satisfaction at the bar. Drink was cheap, Yellowstone whiskey, full quarts then, sold for a dollar a bottle. Old-timers were apt to go on a spree now and then, but were always taken home safely by their friends. There were not many chronic souses. Our few German families made brandy from plums, peaches, and prunes. They distilled a sort of Calvados from cider which made your hair stand on end.

Shortly after I left Mother to join Father in Colorado my mother left the Indian Territory and went to southern Texas to seek a new start. It must have been tough going. She kept boarders, did sewing, worked as a real estate agent, never lost the dream of owning her own ranch. She was a shrewd trader, bought and sold lots in small, growing towns, and accumulated several hundred acres of good farming land, located in Jim Wells County in the middle of a triangle formed by Laredo, Brownsville, and San Antonio. It was a hard dealing area, but she held her own. My sisters worried a good deal about Mother's eccentric ways, as did I. In long letters they gave me news of her buying and selling, and of her friends, who were many. She never changed—iron whims and a will of steel, a habit of following sometimes impossible dreams with an extraordinary ability to irritate more conventional members of the family. Hardly a week passed that I did not receive letters from Nell or Anne giving me detailed news of Mother.

Twenty-five years after I left Kansas and the Indian Territory I was able annually to visit Mother on her ranch. She would never act her age, or tell it. My Aunt Stella was dead, her husband, Uncle Charlie, once wrote to ask Mother if he could come down for deer hunting. Mother asked my advice on my next visit, saying, "You know I love Charlie. He is lonesome now that Stella is dead. We could have a good visit, but don't you think people would talk?" I allowed as how they might get away with it. He and Mother were both nearly ninety!

The region where Mother had her land is an empire now, but then it was thinly settled. Everyone knew and trusted her, for she was an openhearted and openhanded friend to poor whites, some of whom later became immensely rich, and equally friendly to Negroes and to Mexicans. They were all alike to her. She often took in Mexican children when they were ill, or when their mothers were having another child. On one of my visits to her, she had rescued a half-starved Mexican boy who could not speak a word of English. He was soon fat and well. Pepe had the interesting habit of collecting lethal black widow spiders in a beer bottle. One night he informed Mother he had lost the cork! I undressed on top of the bed, but there were no casualties. When it came time for me to catch a night train at a station many miles distant, the grapevine had informed Pepe's parents who came through the mesquite in a dilapidated pickup. The young mother and her new baby were put in the big bed with Pepe; Esteban, the father, drove me to the midnight train, saving my mother a tedious journey. It was like that.

Mother was always somewhat informal about accounts but managed to come out solvent after harvest. I dropped in one time to gossip with the boys at the local bank. The president said, "Mister George, Fanny is overdrawn about nine hundred dollars. There is no hurry, but if convenient, you might take care of it when you go back north."

This I reported to my mother. "Think nothing of it," she remarked. "I'll send a check for the overdraft!" This sort of thing sometimes caused anxiety to my sisters!

Once she said to me mournfully, "I feel we are being smothered here. These people move down from the north and crowd us out." No smoke could be seen from any ranch house, the nearest being four miles away.

A half century after I had left the Indian Territory, my sisters and I, who had had the pleasure of traveling on every continent on various duties, thought it would be nice for Mother to have an organized grand tour of Europe. Raymond-Whitcomb worked out a fine itinerary with books of tickets for trains, sleepers, hotels, meals, excursions, and all the usual things. On her application for a passport she put herself down as only two years old when my elder sister was born!

Everything went fine until she arrived in Florence, where she met an old Spanish couple. What a relief for Mother, as she could speak fair Texas Spanish. They discussed Merino sheep, cattle, horses, crops, and children. They liked one another; finally the Spaniards invited Mother to forget about part of her trip, to go with them to their farm in Andalusia, which she did, for three weeks. One rainy night she turned up in Madrid Central Station to take the express to Paris with ticket and berth reservations dated twenty-one days previously. The train was full. Mother turned loose her Border Spanish on the poor *Wagon Lits* conductor who persuaded someone to give up his accommodation. Two agonized letters from the travel agency came inquiring about Mother's whereabouts. I paid no attention.

Arriving in Paris very late next day after leaving Madrid, Mother went to the Hotel Meurice where again her reservations were three weeks old. At the moment a European Regional American Legion Convention was in progress, the Meurice being entirely full of Yanks! Two former doughboys from Texas made room for her in their quarters. There was much big talk, all three making the usual American complaints about coffee. They then proceeded to the kitchen to brew up some for themselves! As the Legion had the whole place reserved, the management did not object. Mother stayed with the Texans for the best of a week, while they helled around Paris day and night.

Finally, more than three weeks late now, Mother turned up in London inconveniently and unexpectedly where my sister Anne, who had married a starchy English officer, was quietly going mad awaiting her.

I was told in letters that Anne and her husband had planned an evening at the theater for Mother, a First Night. Mother dallied about her dressing. Anne's husband said it was imperative that he and Anne, at least, be on time. They left shillings for a taxi and directions for Mother, and took off. Mother arrived a half hour late in the middle of the first act, with all her new finery—a long, black silk dress of stuff that swished and rattled and a high comb over which she had draped a black lace mantilla she had picked up in Spain. On her feet were red satin shoes purchased on the Rue de La Paix.

With murmurs of disapproval from many she was ushered down to the second row. Trampling over the feet of several cold-eyed dukes and their wives, she took her seat beside my sister. The piece was what the English call a farce. Mother could not understand a word. Thoroughly bored after a few minutes, she whispered to Anne, "I think I'll take off my shoes," and promptly kicked off her new red slippers. Soon she was asleep. During the *entre-acte* when London audiences crowd into the lobby to have a drink or a smoke, or go to the john, she remained seated.

The play finally ended. It happened that when the people in the front row got up at the intermission, they unknowingly pushed Mother's Paris slippers into the little pit that exists in front of most London stages where a scratch orchestra plays "God Save The King." Her slippers were gone, they were nowhere to be seen. What to do? The audience left, the lights were going off, usherettes were collecting discarded programs. Mother was very sweet but determined to retrieve her new merchandise. Anne's husband was livid; Anne was hoping she could die. Finally the manager came, discovered the slippers in the orchestra pit, crawled through the exit and entrance hole beneath the stage, and rescued them. The three went back to the apartment, silently, with mutual homicide in their hearts. Mother could not care a damn less. I am glad I was not at that family party; years later Anne could barely discuss it!

In those later periods whenever I was visiting Mother's ranch I grabbed the opportunity to talk with neighbors about the old days. It enabled me to understand what had transpired in years she had fought it out alone. It had not been easy. There were still thousands of square miles of uncut mesquite in the Rio Grande Valley. The old Camino Real which ran from points in Texas across the Rio Grande, past Saltillo, and on to Mexico City, passed through one section of Mother's land.

One pioneer family were Mother's special friends. They had starved out over on the Nueces River, whereupon they started to look for a new chance farther West. Traveling on Christmas Day with little food, and no meat, they heard squadrons of geese overhead going South. The man lay on his back firing his .30-30 into the flocks. It was a thousand to one chance but a great goose was hit, volplaning down from the sky. They had a good Christmas dinner! One time when every member of this family of six was down with smallpox, an aged Negro, born a slave, who had many scars to prove he had had the disease, nursed the family back to health and strength.

This family one year raised broomcorn, used to make ordinary kitchen brooms. They harvested such a bumper crop it looked as if they could lift their mortgage. But they made the mistake of stacking the harvest too near a dry creek wash where in memory there had been no considerable water. Came a flash flood from heavy rains miles up country. Although there had been no rain near their ranch the water roared down waist high. Not only were the stacks washed away, but also a number of animals. The wife waded into the hazardous flood to seize calves by the ears pulling them to safety. It was not always easy to make a living! This wonderful family stuck by Mother through thick and thin in many hardships and illnesses, and she was a steadfast neighbor to them. It was a comfort to know that in years of severest hardship Mother had such marvelous friends.

In years of our separation letters of my sisters and Mother were a stout support. Packages they sent me, by express, for there was no parcel post then, always of sensible clothing, were a comfort, for I needed them. Nell and

Anne gave me not only news but attempted to keep me from worrying about Mother, but I could read between the lines. I knew they were greatly concerned but were helpless. Mother had to work out life her own way, and undoubtedly did it better than we could have done, had we made the decisions. Both sisters were teaching school and doing well. In my letters east I never referred to the increasing hostility between me and my stepmother.

We plugged along as usual on the ranch on Minnesota Creek. When this land and most of our livestock were sold, we prepared to move to a ranch of raw land in the Payette River Valley of southern Idaho. I loved our mountain region with its variety of terrain and our fine neighbors, but I was soon to be equally devoted to a land vastly different.

PART II
IDAHO
In which I Endeavor To Become a Man

WHEN we moved to the Payette Valley railways were at their peak both in efficiency and in variety and beauty of passenger equipment. Famous trains sped through the Middle West and on to the Pacific, "The Sunset Limited," "The Zephyr," "The Empire Builder," "The Meteor," and later "The Chief" and "El Capitan." Superb Pullman sleepers with inlaid wood and dining cars with chefs equal to any in great cities were on all principal lines.

My father went on ahead to Idaho; I followed. To save money I sat up rather than take a sleeper. For a quarter a dozen bananas were bought which served for food over three nights and three days of the journey to Payette, Idaho, except for one scanty meal had in the diner. A small local train of the Denver and Rio Grande went to Delta, Colorado, then another to Grand Junction, after which a big through-train carried on past Green River, Utah, to Salt Lake City, where the Temple, the Tabernacle and other fine buildings testified to the immense efforts of Mormon pioneers, then on over the Oregon Short Line to Provo, Pocatello, Idaho, and through the Snake River Valley to Payette. Snow covered the desert country. I could hardly believe my eyes at the number of jackrabbit tracks. It did not seem possible—there were millions!

Once I ventured into the dining car. It was a beautiful dream, flowers in vases on each table, white cloths, sparkling silverware, well-dressed people, immaculate waiters, handsome woodwork. No dining car in the East was comparable to those on famous trains of the West. Having previously decided not to go over fifty cents, I studied the menu with care. When I finally ordered, the disgust of the waiter was evident.

Along the route, names of cars from all over the nation provided a lesson in geography. Each locomotive had its own personality. For the first time I saw one of those gigantic double-jointed engines with two cabs and two sets of driving wheels, as my train halted beside it for an hour on a siding. An engineer allowed me to climb into a cab. Canyons east of Salt Lake, where years of heavy pulling had covered the ground with sprinklings of cinders, deep-throated whistles echoing from mountainsides and snowy peaks in the distance, made the journey exciting. I hardly slept on the trip but glued my face to the window lest some station, mountain, or ranch should be passed unseen. There is no music finer than a locomotive's long, baritone whistle in mountainous country.

Arriving in Idaho in a November wet with snow and rain we moved into a tumbledown shack until a simple, square, four-room house could be erected. Our new house was unlined, no plaster, no wallboard. There was no use to complain that it would be as cold as outdoors; there was money for nothing else. Stretched over the studs was a sort of cheesecloth to which was pasted a cheap wall paper that sucked back and forth in the wind. One room we lined with newspapers.

Heat was confined to the kitchen, from the cookstove. As only sagebrush was available to feed the fire, fuel was an acute problem. As winter deepened nearly every ranch woman suffered severely from chilblains. The water bucket was always frozen in the morning. Nearly everyone wrapped warmed bricks in newspaper to help warm the beds.

On Saturdays and Sundays the first priority for me was to go into the hills to cut the best sagebrush that could be found. Nearly every rancher located a place where better specimens grew, keeping the secret as long as he could. After a Chinook wind the ground became so soft I sometimes became stuck with an empty wagon. At night we bundled up in the kitchen, put on an extra pair of sox, and endured. It was impossible in really cold spells, when the temperature went down as low as 30-36 degrees below zero, to maintain any comfort. Father and I wore our hats, my stepmother a shawl over her head. No futile words of complaint were made about the weather for we well knew the same condition existed all along our road.

On outskirts of the irrigated valley were homesteaders. One could see lights in their cabins at night. Hardly any near us ever proved up on their land. It is over sixty-five years now, but the promised water to irrigate orchards and fields they saw in their dreams has never come. Riding through hills looking for heavy stands of sage to cut for firewood, I used to see deserted shacks, monuments to broken hopes. There was a common saying that Uncle Sam bet you a quarter section of land that you could not live on it three years without starving to death.

South of us hills rose gently to a height of land between the Payette and the Snake rivers. It was all sagebrush country; the lovely smell of sage was with us at every season. Between hills which more or less flowed into one another were sand washes, or arroyas, which were dry most of the year. No trees grew except cottonwoods along the Payette River, or those planted on irrigated ranches.

After big snows often came Chinook winds, similar to the Föhn in the Alps. These soft, warm winds, a product of the Japan Current, would melt a foot of snow in a night. In the darkness we could hear arroyas roaring, snow water coming down in a flood. Flimsy bridges on dirt roads would give way, sometimes requiring days to rebuild enough for a light wagon to cross them.

Always at night coyotes came down to the ranches. In years we lived in Colorado and Idaho I cannot recall a night when coyotes were not close by. Their howls disturbed cows and horses who had young, but other stock paid little attention to them. We boys would imitate their different voices, imagining that they responded.

Birds may not have been as plentiful in southern Idaho as in some other regions, but we had many. Especially pleasant were meadowlarks singing in the spring, bobwhite quail, turtle doves, magpies, crows, owls, hawks, a few warblers, and saucy red-winged blackbirds, real sports they were, conscious of their good looks. But we had no mockingbirds. There were a few California crested quails which rapidly increased.

In Idaho we must have been, as in Colorado, on one of the flyways for ducks and geese. In autumn and spring thousands of squadrons passed over us. Their flight patterns were fascinating, one weary leader after another falling back, whose place was quickly taken by another. Melodious honking could be heard at all hours of the day and night. An article in the weekly Spokane *Spokesman-Review* said that ducks and geese shot on the Gulf of Mexico and the Gulf of California still had undigested Canadian food in their crops, which proved they traversed the whole United States, north to south, in one or two flights.

Naturally our first job in Idaho, after we had a roof over our heads, was to clear land, to put in a crop. This tough job largely fell to me, as Father was running a large orchard owned by another man. I was lean and hard, competent to manage the heavy work. Scagebrush presents few difficulties comparable to woodland, but does require much drudgery for horse and man before it yields a harvest. Larger clumps are cut and burned, the remainder attacked with horses and plow. Roots of smaller brush are severed by the plowshare, the brush itself being partly turned under by the plow. Whenever a stone or a large root is struck the plow jumps out of the ground, ofttimes throwing horses upon their knees. This forces the driver to pull back heavy plow and doubletrees ten or fifteen feet to insert the share again in the furrow. A repetition of this process a score of times during ten hours in the field is gruelling labor. Years later I tried to describe putting in raw land in a book, *Reluctant Soil*; the locale was only a mile from our ranch.

The plowing over, the brush, half buried, was gathered

up and burned. In summer, heat was often one hundred and twenty degrees, but if a slight breeze stirred one could work with ease. However I had to watch horses on still days lest they collapse. Heat waves hundreds of feet above the ground made Squaw Butte and the Seven Devils Mountains dance like ships on the sea. There is no easy way to capture the land; it must be taken by force. Between the ages of fourteen and seventeen I cleared eighty acres in the Payette Valley and put it into alfalfa, and I know in my bones the price of new acres. Sometimes I would look up after hours of plowing or grubbing brush to stare at the rim of distant mountains, swearing that some day I would see what lay yonder. But I treasured those acres as I watched them grow.

Southern Idaho presents an amazing number of different soils. Geologically the region is a disturbed sedimentary formation, being part of the bed of a vast inland sea which found outlet through the gorge of the Columbia River. It subsequently suffered volcanic eruption which left deposits of ash. Many lava beds had been thrust up through fissures in the Snake River Valley. Almost every Western valley is different, calling for varied methods of irrigation. Each soil has its idiosyncrasies in taking the water. It requires considerable skill to discover correct adjustments of water to soil. Some ground can be flooded, some can be irrigated only by small ditches, or corrugations, at close intervals.

On our ranch were six or seven different kinds of soil. In the midst of deep volcanic ash formation, hardpan areas bobbed up, and large grease spots, as the ranchers called them, where topsoil was eroded, leaving the hardpan subsoil exposed. These spots were anywhere from ten to one hundred feet in diameter. On these areas water passed over with little effect. A growing field would be as spotted as a leopard with alternating patches of lush alfalfa and bare places where almost nothing grew.

A rancher is partner with the sky, and a very junior partner at that. I soon became sharply aware of weather, for planting, harvesting, hauling, and feeding, and shelter for stock, all depended on sun, rain, snow, cold, or heat. Years later, in cities, habits of watching the weather stayed with me and, I am sure, with other country people who have moved to town. One would say to one's self, "A good day for planting," "Fine time for cutting hay," "Tough for the animals," "No luck for hauling grain," or "A splendid spring for the lambing."

One crop we found easy to raise was potatoes. Idaho was already famous for these. In a sand wash we had there was a perfect strip for planting. We gave them little care for we were busy with haying and clearing land. In harvest time we just rooted them out with a sixteen-inch moleboard plow—over two hundred bushels of enormous smooth specimens. There was little sale for them, so we used what we needed, fed a lot to pigs, and traded some to neighbors for grain.

Our irrigation water came from a big ditch, or canal, over thirty miles long, which had its source in the Payette River far up the Valley near Emmett. Once, along a route traversing a hillside, a large section of the canal gave way. This was a disaster of first magnitude, for crops, men, and animals were dependent upon the water. The whole community rose up to help. There were no large mechanical earth movers in those years. The hillside had to be reduced and a new bed laid for the water. The hardpan was so porous that should the water be turned on again the whole section might once more slough off. To prevent this, strips of canvas were sewn together, coated with tar, then about a foot of earth puddled over this. Luckily, this scheme worked!

It took three weeks to mend the break. Many families camped out near the site, bringing their water in barrels. No one kept track of time, work went on from first light until it was too dark to see.

We employed many tricks to beat summer heat. Nearly every ranch house had a box fitted into a window, on the shady side, with a screen to keep out the flies, where food could be stored for a short time. Over this was often placed a wet cloth. The evaporation made the interior measurably cooler. On windows of sick rooms wet blankets were often hung for the same reason. We sewed a covering of gunny-sacking around water jugs for men working in the fields, which was soaked each time the jugs were filled. I always drank straight out of irrigation ditches, which contained dead squirrels, rats, and mice, but I never contracted typhoid. Hotels in small towns, at the request of demanding guests, sometimes set a block of ice on a box by a window, playing a fan on it, if there was electric power. I suppose it helped some.

There was not much good hunting around us. Up on the Government Reserve in the mountains there were bear, deer, grouse, some elk, and a few antelope, and other game, but in the Payette Valley in vast expanses of sage there were few deer. There were incredible numbers of jackrabbits and ground squirrels, lots of coyotes and many cottontails which made good eating. The jackrabbits we never ate.

Once a coyote drive on horseback was organized. Over one hundred fifty riders were deployed in a big circle about three miles wide. At the sound of a rifle shot we began slowly to approach the center, the idea being to kill a number of these chicken thieves. It did not work. We saw only one coyote who easily avoided us down an arroyo. If the drive had been successful, when we arrived at the center of the circle, any number of riders and horses would probably have been massacred, as we had enough armament for a regiment of Civil War cavalry, .30-30s, .45-70s, .22s, shotguns of every gauge, revolvers, and target pistols. Anyway, it was fun.

Along the Payette River there were numerous small ponds left from high water with a heavy growth of tules, or cattails, to the height of a man. To these came ducks and a few geese which made good shooting. I had no shotgun, but a .22 Marlin repeater and by careful concealment I was able to bring home my share with the other boys. A big goose was a delight and made a feast. We possessed no wading pants so had to stand in the cold water. Boys with shotguns now and then got a goose or duck on the wing. With a rifle I had to wait for a sitting shot.

It was not an easy climate. During summer the dust was as fine as bolted flour. It ran along ruts in front of wheels like water. Approaching wagons could be detected ten or fifteen miles away by dun-colored clouds which drifted slowly across the country like smoke. When high winds came the sun was darkened. During dust storms tumbleweeds and Russian thistles, four and five feet in diameter, careened across the country like stampeding cattle to find lodgement in deep gullies miles away. In winter dust turned to mud, inches deep. When a thaw was on, horses made their way along roads pulling hooves out of the muck with a crack like a pistol shot. There were periods every winter when the mail carriers abandoned roads to take off cross-country with packs on their backs.

A beaver-like passion for work possessed nearly all the ranchers and we were caught up in it. Raw land beckons to men, coaxes out latent capacities for labor, ingenuity, and daring. It is impossible to live near an area of potential wealth without feeling its invitation. The amount of sheer toil men can expend in the presence of virgin soil is almost unbelievable. Men, women, and children give body, mind, and all too often soul to visions of prosperous ranches. In even illiterate and brutish men there is this same release of energy. They arise at night to walk over their acres for the thousandth time, and if on a Sunday they seek rest, they abandoned it to look again at the place where a house, or an orchard, or a garden is to stand.

Our neighbors were all hard up. They were close dealers, for the simple reason that they had little with which to bargain. But they always lent a hand to one another in a day of need. I never knew a person or a family to be turned away if they stopped by wanting food or shelter for man or horse. Names were not asked and no apology was made for lean fare. The boy in the family was by protocol told to water and feed the stranger's horse and no pay was ever expected.

An incident occurred at the beginning of one winter which revealed the basic character of our people. A family and five children were completely burned out on a remote homestead. The neighborhood rose up, built a new house, furnished it, stocked it with food, clothed the children, and forgot about it. They were that sort of people.

As in Colorado, by far the most interesting characters among us were the old-timers, white-haired men and women who had lived out on the edge of things. One old fellow who had known my father in his prosperous years used to come to our ranch occasionally for a few days to get filled up with good food, and to take a breather. He had lived out a fabulous tale, duplicated many times by itinerant prospectors. About 1885 he had discovered a rich lead-silver galena ledge in the Seven Devils Mountains, to the north. Hostile Indians had driven out the whites before he could develop what he was sure was a good mine. The old man had made a careful map of the area showing profiles of nearby mountains, big trees, creeks, and other topographical features. A fire in his cabin some years later burned all his effects—the map was gone. He would work in mines or on ranches in winters, and each summer he explored the country where he had located his ledge. But a forest fire had changed the look of the mountainous vicinity. During twenty summers of searching he could not find the ledge.

But he was never discouraged. As a seasoned miner he knew he had a fortune if he could locate that ledge, and he kept on searching. Death took the old man before his quest was rewarded. The last time I saw him was after breakfast one morning as he started north with his sturdy burro laden with a few days' grub, a packsaddle bulging with equipment, eyes bright and step firm.

Hired men were necessary from time to time when we could spare the expense. Most of them were agreeable. We paid the standard thirty dollars a month for which they worked ten hours a day, helping with morning and evening chores. There was a custom that a hired man slept with a son of the family for houses were not large and seldom did each child have a room of his own. The hired man and I in summer often poured buckets of water over each other in the main irrigating ditch to wash off the grime of the day for there was no bathtub. In winter, on Saturday nights, we took baths in turn, either in a tin washtub or a metal bushel basket. We never loitered in this task.

One able hired man had a distinct drawback, the most stinking feet I ever encountered. Pleas to do something about it went unheeded. In the winter it was awful; in summer I used to sneak out to sleep with the dogs by the big haystack. This fellow insisted on keeping windows shut, claiming night air was bad for the lungs. In all, he was a shocker.

We were not a large grain-producing region, although a fair amount was raised, almost incidentally. Only yesterday every ranch had been raw land. The first attempt to grow crops was nearly always alfalfa. After sagebrush was cleared off, fields and irrigation ditches were laid out, then alfalfa seed was sown, along with oats as a cover crop. Very often a good crop of oats could be harvested while the young alfalfa was taking hold. Also, when old fields were plowed up to reseed, sometimes wheat and barley were planted for a year or two. Hardly ever did one rancher have enough grain to make it profitable for itinerant threshers to visit him. To overcome this several of us stacked our grain on one man's ranch for the threshing.

This was a wonderful time for us youngsters, for what boy does not love the drama of the thresher and its engine? Every able-bodied boy, man, and often women jumped into the task.

The long, swaying, flopping belt from the engine to the separator, the oily smell and roar of the working parts of the machine, the good-humored shouts of the men made it an exciting occasion. There was one boy with the thresher crew, no older than some of us, who had the job of standing by the mouth of the separator where sharp, revolving knives cut the binder twine and a moving canvas belt pulled straw with its headed grain into the belly of the apparatus. From time to time sweet clover with long woody stalks would clog up the mouth of the separator. The boy's job was skillfully to thrust in a stick to stop the intake until the revolving knives could clear out the obstruction. That seemed to me the height of mechanical achievement. The boy was a hero to me! I dared not speak to him.

Thresher crews were expert judges of food and well they might be. Most ranchers' wives were good cooks and they all joined in providing food in threshing and haying time. There were fried chicken, sweet and Irish potatoes, peas, beans, lettuce, biscuits, salt-rising bread, chocolate and coconut cake, coffee with rich cream, milk, canned fruit, and preserves, with dill pickles, sauerkraut, onions, radishes, parsnips, and turnips on the table, and pies—peach, apple, cherry, custard, mince, squash, pumpkin, and others. The women counted in quarts canned fruit and preserves they had made and stored in their cellars. They could tell to the last Mason jar how many hundred containers they had of peaches, pears, plums, berries, apricots, cherries, and jellies.

At loaded tables, during our harvest meals we boys could be forgiven for boasting of our mothers and in taking pride in the prowess of our men.

Mutual aid was practiced in our valley, for it was our only way. By snowfly each rancher had repaid the others for their help so that no money changed hands. Of course the thresher crew proper were paid hard cash.

The dominating feature in lives of us ranchers was neither persons, nor weather, nor animals, nor crops, but the immense gray waste of sage above the big irrigation ditch. Between this canal and the Payette River to the north lay a patchwork of fields of alfalfa or occasional plantings of oats, wheat, or barley, young orchards, and here and there uncut areas of brush not yet brought under the plow. To the south all was different. A superficial glance would indicate that the virgin brushland was monotonous, devoid of character, of a uniform drabness, but this appearance differed throughout each day and season, and between light and darkness.

On rising from sleep a rancher's first thought in summer was the irrigation. The set of the water was changed each morning, not only for reasons of economy in order to cover thirsty fields as soon as possible, but also to prevent washing away of topsoil caused by frequent breaks in lateral ditches during hours of night. Next, one fed the stock, but always eyes were turned to a contemplation of the great sweep of sage as far as one could see south and east and west. Its colors, texture, and grim beauties increased as one lived near it, always somber, always changing to the eye. In senses more than sheerly geographical it was our reference point.

At sunrise, rays stealing through gaps in mountains eastward sought out higher rises, clothing them in silver light, while night continued to linger on, flowing from one arroyo into another, deepening their gloomy demeanor. Only slowly did hot blasts from above blend all in a mauve sameness.

Blazing noondays generally found the sky a fierce brass shield when the sage seemed positively to crouch beneath the flailing from overhead. Even as mountain dwellers look up from toil to rest a moment, their eyes seeking solace from peaks against the horizon, so we would study, not the checkerboard of ranches toward the river, but involuntarily let our gaze roam over sage-clad hills.

On days of threatened storm, clouds swept over the deserty land, whose shadows in everchanging intensities, never static, gave a deceitful concept of distances over the rising and falling of hills, separated by gentle depressions of the swales. Under the fluidity and mutations of cloud, the waste, so often inanimate and unmoving, came alive. On moonless nights all was dead and very black. But always, save when wrapped in snow, it breathed off a perfume—clean, astringent, aromatic, the one delicate element in a savage landscape.

Along bottoms of bigger arroyos were sand washes made by torrential runoffs when Chinook winds melted snow. These dry stream beds reflected sunlight as from the surface of a mirror, making crooked ribbons descending the long, low hills, pallid, whitish, and hard on the eyes.

At sundown one could easily have the illusion that night came up from the waste to meet the sky, rather than otherwise, for thin splashes of darkness spread over the landscape unevenly, giving forth a sinister aspect. This austere area was never friendly, at times positively hostile. No jubilant notes of gaity were ever forthcoming such as one encounters in valleys where the hand of man had brought bright flowers and grasses and trees to embellish nature. The waste was neutral, willing to be employed, to receive seed, to nurture crops, but it never helped, and at moments could be actively reluctant.

Over most of this expanse there was only the sparest grass cowering near the stems of brush, rich and nourishing and relished by sheep, whether green or dry. Now and then occurred small patches in some wide hollow where verdure came up rank and green, a treasure for hungry animals.

Silence was the accustomed mood of land above the big ditch. Few birds sang there. But, even as in timber country where on the stillest days could be heard the swoosh of slowly moving air in treetops, so in the low sage, when there was only a slight breath of wind, the waste had its own distinctive voice, a gentle sibilance, varied, as a quiet ventilation going up the valley sifted through differing forms of vegetation. At night one could recognize without sight the nature of nearby brush by sounds among the tiny branches.

Rabbits and squirrels were ever near, but often unseen. Nevertheless, one was aware of bright eyes watching every move, alert, in vigil against hazard from any quarter. And at night there was always the chattering and yapping of the coyotes.

The main irrigation canal had steep banks, too wide and deep to cross on foot or horseback. Crude bridges were constructed every five or six miles. Sagebrush land above the cultivated ranches in autumn and early spring provided a feeding ground for several hundred thousand sheep, which, as cold weather began, in bands of two thousand to twenty-five hundred, were slowly herded down from Government Reserves in the mountains. When snows covered wild grass sheep were driven over the bridges to ranches where their owners had purchased hay for winter feeding. Sage was worn down to bare stumps and stems as bands of sheep converged on the bridges, all bushes having little flags and banners of yellowing wool attached to them. When snow melted away in spring a quick crop of grass sprang up in lands above the big ditch. Then sheep reversed their autumn journey to feed in the great wastes until lambing time was past. Loads of hay were carried up to feed in this period when lanterns burned all night as herders stood by to help ewes in difficulty. Afterward, in slow stages, the bands were directed again to summer pastures in the highlands. The big ditch was a dividing line between two ways of life, two modes of husbandry.

A curse threatens nearly every irrigated region—seepage. Sometimes this does not appear until years after irrigation is laid on, or it may come in a short time. Water from main and lateral ditches soaks down until it strikes a harder layer of subsoil, gradually to emerge at lower levels into the open air. As water subs up it brings with it alkaline and other mineral salts which, on evaporation, leave a crust of these lethal substances on the surface, killing nearly all vegetation, leaving desolate, scabrous patches, often many acres in extent. Alfalfa fields and orchards perish under this blight—a tragedy for the owner. Flooding and deep drainage ditching sometimes help clear away these deposits, but generally the damage is permanent. Our large pond, used for skating, was formed by a dike across a low arroyo.

This backed up water of the big ditch to form a lake of some hundred acres. Suddenly, within the space of one summer, underground water following hardpan strata ruined fertile fields of garden soil on the lower reaches. Landowners in an irrigated valley fear seepage like they dread the devil.

Water is the lifeblood in an arid land, and greatly treasured. The usual legal allotment of water in an organized irrigation district is one miner's inch of water per acre. This is calculated as the amount in a still ditch, which, with a free fall, passes over a trapezoidal weir at a depth of one inch. Waste water running off from a ranch onto lower land can be filed on by a legal process giving a permanent water right which is a valuable asset.

It may not be so in cities, but on the land spring brings with it a burst of fresh life and hope and energy. Neglected corners are cleaned up, ditches repaired, new roofs put on, fences restrung, old posts replaced, dreams revived. Sluggish cattle, who have moved all winter as if half dead, rush about tails in air. Hair is shed from winter coats of horses and cows. Singing periods in school are longer and louder. Love notes are secretly passed between boys and girls or hidden in textbooks where they can easily be found. As we kids walked along roads to school we saw the ancient yearly miracle of plant and animal emerging from the frost, snow, and immobility of winter. Squirrels and rabbits came out of their holes. Coyotes, lean and hungry, came in from the waste, their faded hair falling off leaving almost naked patches on their sides. Wild onions, cowslips, violets sprang up among the sage. Scrub willows along ditches first showed leaves, light yellow and greenish, shining in the sun and sticky with sap. In orchards, first apple, then peach, and afterward plum and prune trees began to leaf out. In a few weeks the perfume of flowering fruit trees was along our route. This was an anxious time. A few hours of late frost could kill a crop and bring despair to many homes. Sparrows and robins returned and four sorts of blackbirds, warblers and especially meadowlarks with songs which someway lifted the heart of the dourest rancher. Spring renewed our existence; we were close to the soil, felt its stirring, old grudges were forgotten as we entered once more into dreams of fertile fields and felt the quickening of blood in our creatures.

No season, not even harvest time, so enlivened us as did spring. Sharp responses gave way to better manners, and scolding to laughter. Stubborn land which had long defied taming was attacked with fresh hope and vigor. Nothing seemed impossible.

On cold autumn mornings often occurred a peculiar phenomenon. Over close-cut alfalfa fields a fairy lacework of spider webs covering large areas slowly lifted and fell in low, billowing waves as air currents along the ground disturbed this wide, thin, silken fabric with droplets of dew and frost sparkling in the early sun, the work of multitudes of tiny workers.

In spring and autumn when hot days were followed by frigid nights the course of the Payette would be covered with a white mist, as if a great jug of milk were spilled up near Squaw Butte to flow in the depths of the valley as the stream made its crooked way to the Snake River. This narrow ribbon of mist lingered until the sun, like a great skyborne cat licked it up as the day grew older.

A tragedy lost me one of the best friends of my youth. Roscoe Bean was a good worker, had an above-average mind and athletic prowess known for miles up and down the Valley. He was a natural leader, had judgment far beyond his years. His mother was a Swede who could barely speak English. She was possessed of physical beauty and an integrity of character which she passed on to her children. Roscoe was the best horseman, skater, ballplayer, and hunter among us. One day on the alkali flats near the Payette River, on a duck-hunting expedition, his shotgun slipped through the slats of a sulky he had made. The firing pin was driven into the shell with the full load penetrating Roscoe's body.

Roscoe was taken to a shack nearby where Dr. Drisdale

and neighbor women nursed him for a week until his death. Each evening after work some fifty friends would ride in to sit in the salt grass passing to one another news of the wounded boy's progress in the past day and night. We would ride back to our ranches late in the evening with heavy hearts. Not much could be done for him. The grave injuries finally overcame his natural strength; we were properly sobered and saddened, for Roscoe was the most promising one among us.

Down the road toward town three quarters of a mile lived an Irish Catholic family named Meehan, wonderful people. Three older sons worked away in lumber and mining camps and on railway construction. A grown girl taught school up in the Seven Devils Mountains at Long Valley. One boy, my age, lived at home. We went to and returned from school together. In that family it was all for one and one for all. Came hay time the three older boys returned to help, for as a family they were a team—they meshed. Each year more land was cleared. In two years an almost derelict ranch that several previous owners had failed to improve was in excellent shape.

The Meehan boy on long walks to and from school passed on to me instruction in Catholic ways and doctrine he received from the itinerant priest who served several parishes in the Valley. We shared ideas and possessions. He was a good shot and we frequently hunted rabbits together on Sunday afternoons. So often out there one saw how a family, pulling in unison, could put together homes, ranches, herds, almost anything to which they set their hands. The opposite was also true.

There were numerous fights among us boys—none very serious. I had no great prowess, although I was not a bad wrestler for my weight. In my first serious fight I was properly clobbered. Most ranchers and their children are humane in treatment of animals. On the road to school one day after big rains a man with a heavy load was badly stuck. He was unmercifully and unreasonably beating his horses. Any decent person would have objected which I did. The enraged driver came at me like a gorilla. He was twice as big, and stronger, so that I hardly got in a blow. He knocked me down a few times, finally pushing me along the slippery road, loaded with curses and a kick in the behind. On arriving at school the teacher cleaned up my face, rubbed turpentine on my cuts, and approved of my action. It took me some years to learn one cannot, alone, correct all the world's shortcomings. But I do not repent me of speaking up for the horses.

Movies did not exist in the Payette Valley. Once I went for a day to Caldwell, about thirty miles south of us through low sagebrush hills. There were two small theaters and I sat twice through each showing. I saw a comedy, probably an early Mack Sennett, and several French films, all tinted blue, by Pathé, and a film by a company named Kalem. I was enthralled. They depicted French ceramic and metalworking factories. Entrance fee was ten cents; the machine stuttered, films frequently broke, but what a day!

There were no vacations and little of what is called recreation in our Valley. Never having had it, we never missed it. We had baseball teams at school which now and then played other clubs, but distances prevented much of this. We never had a fully uniformed team; we played in our overalls. Some of the boys were splendid athletes. Later, when a number, by sheer grit, went to college, almost every one of them played on varsity teams. Work and school seemed to fulfil our needs.

One young man from a small town north of us, Weiser, became famous as a baseball player. A scout from Washington, D.C., came out, saw him play and recruited him. He was Walter Johnson, for a generation one of the great athletes and gentlemen of the sports world.

A neighbor had a phonograph, the only one along our road. It had a big horn shaped like a morning glory, painted in vivid colors. We children would be very quiet as the twelve records were played, "Uncle Josh at the Husking Bee," and others. There was one piece, "The Moon

Shines Tonight on Pretty Red Wing," which in those days I thought was the loveliest song I had ever heard!

Every family had two possessions: a Bible, not much read but carefully preserved, and either a Sears, Roebuck or a Montgomery Ward catalogue. The boys spent hours reading descriptions of tools, farm implements, and especially of guns, saddles, and harness. To people denied access to towns with ample shops these mail-order houses were a blessing. Many women carefully preserved yearly catalogues of seed houses reading with love about flowers and looking at colored pictures, for they had little time to cultivate gardens of their own. The soil was generally hostile and the climate rugged, and duties laid heavy claim upon a woman's time and energies.

We did have the intinerant medicine shows common throughout the West. About every year one came to our Opera House for ten days or two weeks. The troupe generally consisted of a boss man who made the selling pitch about his wares, also a sort of a roustabout messenger boy, and a comedian, banjo player, singer and all-around entertainer. The shows offered a variety of articles, highly scented powders and perfumes for the ladies, many kinds of medical soaps and lotions, a sure cure for tapeworm (a very popular item), nostrums for piles, deafness, lost manhood, Bright's disease, toothache, back sprain, spavin cure for horses, worm medicine for dogs, and a positive preventive for hog cholera.

Medicine-show men had tricks to increase trade, generally some form of popularity contest for the most personable local girl or woman. Several candiates would be put up, supported by the young bucks. A certain number of "lady" votes were given out with each dollar's worth of goods purchased. Competition was ruthless, encouraged by skillful gossip by the medicine-show man. High words and not seldom fistfights occurred. The shows left behind considerable enmity; seeds of discord were sown which bore fruit in the following months. These shows took many hundreds of dollars away from our few stores.

While I was working and living on the ranch in Idaho there occurred the famous trial of Moyer, Haywood, and Pettibone which threw a young prosecutor into national prominence, William E. Borah. The Western Federation of Miners had become dominated by criminals. The Union had a hatchet man, Harry Orchard, who dynamited the railway station at Independence, Colorado, killing over twenty persons. They also blew up the Bunker Hill and Sullivan Mine in the Coeur d'Alene country. Later Orchard dynamited Governor Steuncnberg of Idaho; they were rough. Harry Orchard turned State's evidence, to tell a gruesome story. Borah did a brilliant job. Big Bill Haywood eventually escaped to Russia where he lived out a miserable life. Years later I saw him once on the Red Square walking with Trotsky, looking very dejected.

We subscribed regularly to weekly editions of the Spokane *Spokesman-Review,* which gave regional news of the Columbia River Basin, called the Inland Empire, but in order to keep up with exciting trial news we ordered also the Boise *Statesman.* A number of ranchers came in each evening to read the news.

William E. Borah became a hero to us boys. Even before the case against Orchard, Moyer, Haywood, Pettibone, and the killers of the Western Federation of Miners, he had achieved local fame in the murder trial of Paul Cocoran. Corcoran's alibi was that he was several miles away at the time of the murder. Some State's witnesses, however, swore they saw him near the locality of the crime standing on top of a fast moving boxcar, with a rifle, and that he had jumped off the train at Burke. The conductor and brakeman of the train testified for the defense that with the speed of the train, and the rough and crooked roadbed in the canyon, it would have been impossible for any man to do this, that he would have been thrown off and killed. Whereupon Borah blew up Corcoran's alibi by riding the route under the same conditions, carrying a rifle, and by landing on his feet when he jumped off at Burke. In Idaho one need not have been a Republican to admire Borah!

Harry Orchard who had placed the bomb that killed Governor Steunenberg on New Year's Eve 1905 became a model prisoner and very religious. He was serving a life term, but as a special dispensation for good conduct was allowed to live outside the walls of the prison in a small house, and to raise chickens.

Ranch women of southern Idaho had special burdens to bear. It was impossible to keep a house tidy because of dust and mud. Most ranchers were forced to use ditch or well water that was often strongly alkaline. Sagebrush was our only fuel and it took an enormous amount to do baking or washing. Kitchens were always littered with bark and dry leaves each time a fresh lot was fed into hungry stoves. Rustling water and wood was often left to the women. They were a grand lot, many quite handsome in their husbands' old hats and mackinaws. In their steady eyes and brown faces there was plenty of character. They knew life, they liked it, and were unafraid; they had guts.

Wives had to remain at home alone with children, often seeing no one else for weeks, while husbands were away on other ranches or worked in mining or timber camps, to earn enough money to feed and clothe the family, to buy seed or animals. The women's tasks were never done. Long after drowsy families were asleep wives attended sick children and ailing animals, darned and knitted, tucked away incubator chicks, set the bread, made arrangements for breakfast, scrubbed milk utensils and prepared for another day. It was not an easy problem for either man or wife. One occasionally saw a good division of labor but such examples were rare. Ranch wives with sheer heroism stood beside their men of the Santa Fé, the Overland and the Oregon trails, and in all the little flats, valleys, and mesas of the West.

Women never failed to help one another when there was sickness or when a new baby was to arrive. They knew the processes and hazards of birth, for had they not been midwives to the animals? At least half the boys and girls along our road had been born without an assisting doctor, the neighbor women lending a hand.

Wives exchanged flowers, vegetable seeds, and clothes for grown-ups and children. Some families had relatives in the East who sent good used clothing which was a blessing. They traded recipes and cuttings from plants. When possible they read a little. Our magazines went the rounds, especially among the women, until they were worn out. The State Library sent a box of assorted books each month to remote communities which requested this service. Five or six ranch wives trusted me to draw out books for them to read to children.

Bread was baked in each home, for we seldom went to the village. We made our own yeast, using a fermented potato ball. My stepmother was very skillful at this. Hardly a week passed but some woman "lost her potato ball," as the ferment became so diluted it would not work. She would borrow a lump from us, mix it thoroughly with mashed potatoes, and she was again in business. In addition to regular household work ranch wives did hair cutting for all the family. For years I never visited a barber.

Our valley was a masculine world. The land had its own beauty, but was severe, and in cloudy weather the sagebrush waste was gloomy and hostile. Mountains to the north and east made a savage rim to our lower country, a man's land, to be explored and broken. Work in irrigated regions was hard for men, for women it was the limit of their strength and, in some cases, beyond their powers. Children helped, but even this aid was not always sufficient. Ranch wives did not complain; if they failed beneath their burden they expressed, mutely, a sense of shame. Men did not intend to be harsh, but both man and wife were caught in a situation from which there was no escape this side of years of hard labor.

We were an undemonstrative people. Without doubt there was deep love between couples who had married in the fullness of beauty and strength in younger years. Although in the family there was pride in the prowess of husband, wife, parent, or boys and girls, there was little outward tenderness. Men would come back from months'-long absences to make ready money working in mines, lumber camps or railway construction, arrive home, nod to a wife, smile, perhaps place earnings on the kitchen table, and go out to animals and fields.

The claims of land and stock upon our people left little time for dalliance. I only knew one case of a married man seducing another man's wife, a situation which lasted briefly and was soon healed.

If relations between man and wife were overly austere, dry, and given to little warmth, full strength and beauty of home love was often evident between mothers and children. When a mother placed a work hardened hand upon the head or shoulder of a questioning child and looked into his eyes, one saw the depths of affection and a willingness to sacrifice for this offspring, the fruit of her body. The kids loved and respected their mothers in return. Of course we were a human grouping and not all fathers and mothers were devoted to their boys and girls, but most of them were. Home life was slim, but genuine, much was unspoken, much felt.

Animals gave much to ranch people in addition to a basic utility as workers and givers of milk, hides, and food. A ranch boy develops a close kinship with them inasmuch as his clothes, his hair, and his body take on mingled smells of the corrals, a not unpleasant mixture; cows and horses and their offspring each have an individual odor. At school it was quite easy to distinguish boys from village homes from ones from the outlying countryside. Ranch girls were well scrubbed, free from the strong scent of the boys, but they never reproached us as it was an understood part of our life.

On black, icy mornings at milking time thick winter fur of big horses provided an excellent place to warm hands. From time to time fatigue in aching fingers could be relieved by thrusting them deep into the warm flanks of the gentle cows. Ranch cats gathered at milking time to catch warm jets of milk direct from the udders, with no spilling! It was remarkable how quickly kittens caught on to this trick!

The breeding of livestock is vital to ranchers. One has only to look at scrubby cattle and horses in many localities to see what neglect brings. Some horses, burros, and mules, brought to North America by the Conquistadores, ran away to become wild, others were captured by Indians. Indians did little in developing their stock, a practice resulting in their cayuses being generally skinny, light weight, about twelve to fourteen hands high. After the Civil War farmers and ranchers of the West began to take serious interest in improving all varieties of their stock.

Few ranchers could afford a purebred stallion. In Idaho we preferred Belgian, Percheron, or Suffolk Punch for breeding. These were often purchased for $2,000-$2,200 from McLaughlin Brothers in Omaha. To lighten the load ranchers would purchase fifty- to one-hundred-dollar shares. A trusted man was given charge of the stallion, who made rendezvous at certain specified ranches during the week. A charge of twenty to twenty-five dollars was charged for servicing a mare, to be paid after it was certain she was "with child." Crossing these fine stallions with grade mares quickly produced magnificent beasts.

We had a mixture of mules and horses. The mule is strong, can take heat and privation better than a horse, and is more intelligent about food and drink. A mule, no matter how hungry or thirsty, will seldom eat or drink until he founders; a horse will. The horse, with larger hoofs, is somewhat better on muddy roads.

Handsome Missouri mules, almost black, with lovely white noses, standing sixteen and a half hands high, the beloved of Army transport and dirt-moving contractors throughout the world until automotive equipment came in, are curious biological phenomena. The mule is achieved by breeding a horse mare to a jack. The jack is a chunky, knobby, unprepossessing animal, originally from Spain. He has little affection for horses, but he does his job. The mare is generally placed in a shallow pit in order for the jack to function properly, for he is less tall than the mare.

After the little mule is born, the mare, in a corral with others who have horse foals, seems somewhat embarrassed. Her mule baby tickles her with his long ears when nursing. Among adult mules and horses, almost always mules are thrust aside as socially unacceptable. A separate feeding rack is generally provided for them.

Because mules are hybrids they cannot reproduce. To secure jacks for breeding purposes they must come from "Jeannettes," true female mules, somewhat bigger than our Western burros, but not as large as horses.

On the ranch we were never able to achieve such a measure of affection from mules as from horses. Mules are far more reserved, having all the characteristics of a self-conscious person.

We raised some beautiful horses by breeding our mares to Belgian and Percheron stallions. Some at two years weighed twenty-two hundred pounds and stood sixteen and a half hands high. While in Colorado we had several lighter horses for buggy or saddle; in Idaho we only had one saddle horse.

Over the whole of Western ranch country were posted bills telling the qualities of different stallions and jacks, where and when they could be found. In our valley there were a Nero, a Charlemagne, a Pedro, and several other stallions, and a jack with the comic name of Come Now!

One stallion we especially liked, a sorrel Belgian, had a tracheotomy operation. He had suffered a stoppage in his breathing apparatus. A clever veterinary surgeon had inserted a silver tube with a screen on it. The giant horse seemed to have no inconvenience whatever. It is the only tracheotomy I encountered in years of dealing with horses.

When it was possible we boys gathered at horse sales. Ranchers were in general good judges of horseflesh. The first thing a man did who was thinking of buying was to open a horse's mouth to look at his teeth. They could then tell the animal's age within a year. From this custom derives the old saying, "Don't look a gift horse in the mouth," for who would wish to insult a generous donor! The second examination was of horses' legs to feel for puffy places which indicate a spavin. A light horse for riding, or for a buggy, would bring about one hundred dollars, a heavy draft horse of good age and condition from one hundred fifty to two hundred dollars.

On most deals our neighbors were wholly trustworthy. I would never hesitate to buy or sell land, cattle, sheep, grain, or hay with them. When it came to trading or selling horses it was different. We would not hesitate to misrepresent, to drive a hard bargain. I have been cheated and have done some sharp tricks myself. It was an accepted custom, a sort of game!

There are unpleasant but necessary tasks in every calling. All the ranch boys participated in caring for animals. There are some delightful moments in dealing with horses, cows, their offspring, and even with pigs, but other aspects are not so easy to take. I helped in castration of calves, colts, and pigs, but I avoided butchering. Maybe I was yellow, but I never took part in that for the animals, many of which I had raised from infancy, were like pets or friends. I never felt this way about chickens, geese, turkeys, or ducks. They never seemed to me to be people in the sense the four-footed beasts did.

There was one rather grim aspect of ranching. If one loves animals, or at least respects them, a persistent problem lies in what to do about the very old and feeble, the unfit, and the badly diseased. Few ranchers can afford, no matter how much a horse may be loved, to keep him on indefinitely. The most humane solution, no matter how sad it made us, was to take such an animal a mile or so into the sage above the big ditch and put a 30-30 bullet into his brain. It was a painful task, but necessary in view of all considerations. Coyotes in a few days picked the bones clean. We boys in our rabbit hunting avoided skeletons of animals we had known. The greatest offense, universally acknowledged, was to neglect a horse, who had given good service, in days of old age or infirmity.

Although I was reared amid dozens of horses I never had any animal of my very own, except cats and dogs, until we were ranching in Idaho. My father gave me a colt from his excellent saddle mare, a golden sorrel, as delicate as a gazelle, gentle, but she would never allow a human being to touch her. All the other horses and foals, mules and burros would crowd about us, but never she. I did not know why she was so shy. She was a fairy princess, clean, shining, and beautiful, with two white-stockinged feet and a handsome star in her forehead. I loved her with all my heart.

One hard summer when feed was scarce we fenced in thirty acres of sagebrush, with some good grass on it, to use for the non-working horses and their foals. We finished the job one day about sunset. When corral gates were opened, some twenty horses and foals exploded out, running into the sunset. They didn't see the new barbed-wire fence, two or three squarely hitting it at the same moment. The wires sang and broke. These animals received some direct cuts. My exquisite filly had a wire snap back and cut her deeply in the neck and chest. Some animals seem to know when they are mortally wounded. Although I had never laid a hand on her, she came slowly to stand against me as her life's blood poured down her breast. I held her head in my arms until her legs gave way and she lay down to die. There are sorrows too deep for tears!

The one spot of excitement in the long sun-flailed days of summer was the coming of the Danish mail carrier, driving his little white wagon. It is hard to exaggerate the importance of mail to people in isolated places. Usually he came by our place at about two thirty in the afternoon. From where I worked at the plowing I could see the dust of his coming for a mile up the road. It always quickened my pace. If I were where I could, I always watched to see whether he stopped at our box. My sisters Nell and Anne and my mother were faithful correspondents during years of our separation. They never failed to send Christmas boxes of needful things, by express, or did they forget my birthday. Letters and magazines which came by mail carrier were our one link with the outside world. I hold that Dane in special affection.

Except in rare cases, such as one German neighbor, we were not expert farmers. Not yet had knowledge and techniques developed by agricultural colleges, county agents, and farmers' institutes become widespread and accepted. Dirt farmers are conservative; they resist change. Rotation of crops, hybrids, care of animals, storage of crops, proper fertilization, upgrading of stock were talked about and most often dismissed as something beyond them. Young people who took courses in agriculture were often discouraged. There was a joke about a lad who came back from one of the "cow colleges," as we called them. He said, "Father, if we boiled that corn hogs could digest it easier and faster." The old father replied, "What's time to a hog?"

It is one thing by sheer brawn and willpower to clear raw land, it is quite another to develop it into a fruitful source of yearly crops. We were also backward in the skillful use of tools. Our blacksmith was the one man in the valley genuinely adept with mechanical devices. By sheer work, long and hard, we did accomplish some good results. We could have done more, and faster, if we had applied available knowledge and made our heads save our heels.

School, as in Colorado, was excellent. There was one man teacher for the eighth grade and all four classes of high school. Eighth-grade examination papers at that time in Idaho were not read locally, but by some office in Boise. Our teacher was so good that I was able to win the best mark in the state. As a result, a scholarship to the preparatory department of The College of Idaho at Caldwell was awarded me. Because we were short of money, and because I was needed at home, it was necessary to decline.

These country schoolteachers had a touch of genius, or was it sheer devotion? To teach every subject in the four years of high school and all in the eighth grade required close planning of the school day.

We children relished periods set aside for recitations of poetry. We were allowed to choose any piece, but generally we selected one with rhythm and melody as they were more easily remembered. Older poets were our favorites. Everyone worked hard to finish classes early, even giving up half the noon hour and some recesses, for practice. It often happened that listeners learned a piece and recited it better than the pupil who had chosen it.

When our teachers felt that we were ready, we held a Parents' Night. Several fathers and mothers could not read or write but listened with pride as sons and daughters performed. We were not an especially sensitive lot, but some way we felt we must do our best for the elders. This feeling was never mentioned, but it was deep. Modest prizes were given, generally books purchased from the meager salary of our teacher. This man who conducted all the high school and eighth grade received seventy dollars a month.

Boys and girls recited all the familiar pieces: "The Curfew Shall Not Ring Tonight," "Horatio at the Bridge," "The Wreck of the Hesperus," "Sparticus to the Gladiators," and often selections from *The Lady of the Lake, The Vision of Sir Launfal* and *In Memoriam.* Lowell, Whittier, Bryant, Holmes, and Longfellow were much favored and occasionally a bit from a modern writer. Once a boy gave us "The Face on the Bar Room Floor" by Robert W. Service, but it was frowned upon. Almost every year some lad recited Henley's "Invictus" and some girl chose Shelley's "To a Skylark." Bryant's "To A Waterfowl," Browning's "Rabbi Ben Ezra," and Burns's "John Anderson, My Jo," were much relished as was Thomas Hood's "I Remember, I Remember."

One Parents' Night was outstanding. A girl rendered Lanier's "Marshes of Glynn" without missing a syllable. A strapping boy bellowed out "Gunga Din." The applause was so vehement that our teacher allowed him to recite "The Road to Mandalay" as an encore, which he did well.

Mostly we loved patriotic poems, Whitman's "O Captain! My Captain" and "I Hear America Singing," Hosmer's "O

Beautiful, My Country," Longfellow's "Sail On, Sail On, O Ship of State," and Whittier's "Barbara Frietchie." I gained a lean fourth place one night with Patrick Henry's fiery words to the Virginia House of Burgesses—"Give me liberty or give me death!"

All this was more than fun. We became acquainted in a small way with good writing, developing a taste which, for some, persisted. Teachers above and beyond the line of duty planted a healthy ferment in our otherwise rather humdrum existencc.

Music in our schools was a boon to us. There was always a session in each school day from a wonderful book. It had old favorites—"Listen to the Mocking Bird," "I Am Thinking Now of Hallie," "The Harp That Once Through Tara's Halls," "Oft in the Stilly Night," "Flow Gently, Sweet Afton," "Swanee River," "Old Black Joe" and all our national patriotic songs. And there was one with words:

> The sod school house in the far, far West
> Where the prairie blossoms blow
> Shall be at last as truly blest
> As the log ones long ago.

Some girls, genuinely good singers, used to perform at church sociables, strawberry festivals, graduations, and community occasions.

We all knew western songs often sung at the lunch break —the more mournful the better! One girl could sing all the verses of "O Bury Me Not on the Lone Prairie," toward the end it ran:

> O bury me not on the lone prairie-e-e
> Where the wild coyote will howl o'er me
> Where no hand will plant forget-me-not.
> O bury me not in this lonely spot!
>
> She's been in my dreams, But he ended there
> They paid no heed to his dying prayer
> In a lonely grave just six by three
> They buried him there, on the lone prairie-e-e.

The teacher who was a good singer and piano player tried to train us in part singing. Girls quickly learned, but boys were no good; we were either too shy, or just plain dumb.

We children were not over bright but the ambition which drove our parents to tame wild land spurred us in our eagerness to learn. If lessons were done early our teachers would often read to us. For those of us who finally attended universities it was a case of the tortoise and the hare, perseverance rather than any marked intelligence.

Long evenings made studying easy for there were no distractions. Work in the field, chores, and reading at night were the routine week after week. From the state library books I received my introduction to G. K. Chesterton. Years later I sat at table with him and Ramsey MacDonald when they received honorary degrees from the University of Edinburgh. Chesterton asked eagerly about men and women who had read his *Heretics* and *Orthodoxy* on the wastes of southern Idaho.

In remote places boys are often isolated of body, but not of spirit. Among our subscriptions to magazines were *Everybody's*, *Munsey's*, *The Century*, and the weekly Spokane *Spokesman-Review*. I read every line of them and borrowed books from scanty shelves of neighbors. The building of the Panama Canal and the great lawsuit culminating in a fine of $29,240,000 against the Standard Oil Company were followed in detail, as was William Randolph Hearst's revelation that Senator Foraker had been connected with Standard Oil in an unethical manner. I was an intense patriot and found it almost unbelievable that a senator could be dishonest. Another interest which was pursued closely in the papers and magazines was national conservation. My first knowledge of William E. Borah was his exoneration in land fraud cases.

We who lived close to deserts, forests, mines, and streams found a special concern in the Pinchot-Ballinger controversy over ways and means of safeguarding national resources. Land frauds in the west reached gigantic proportions. Political campaigns were discussed whenever men met one another on the dusty roads. Whether you knew the driver or not you stopped and talked with him.

Girls among our schoolmates were an upstanding lot, and capable. They helped one another make dresses and care for their hair and faces. There were no cosmetics, but plenty of soap. Wind, sun, sound food, and sleep gave them a robust charm. Some would be considered outstanding beauties in any grouping. There was little about ranch work unknown to them. In haying time they worked in the field, could feed stock, irrigate, tend bees, saddle and harness a horse, milk a cow, or feed pigs and chickens as expertly as their brothers. From infancy they followed mothers in household chores, learning to clean, mend, cook, wash, iron, and care for animals and younger children.

There were no nervous breakdowns due to adolescent mix-ups about sex, for they were given, by mothers and other older women, knowledge of every aspect of conception and birth among both animals and humans. And they had before their eyes the open lessons of barns and corrals. Ongoing life on a ranch would cease without a knowledge and acceptance of the processes of reproduction. To plead ignorance or over-delicacy would not be modesty, but stupidity. In fact one teenage girl learned midwifery to the extent that she was often called as a helper at times of childbirth.

The girls were all shapes and sizes, blondes and brunettes, none unseemly fat. Some plain ones were nevertheless among the most attractive due to steady eyes, clear complexion, even if browned and freckled by the sun. Their speech was of a better quality than that of the boys who used slang and sloven language. The girls took pride in a proper use of words. They had the coquetry native to women, pretending contempt for projects and ideas of boys, but they were always quick to assist us in repainting the small school library, skinning off the new baseball diamond, or decorating for a Parents' Night.

As with us boys they worked away from home when they

could be spared. What they did not learn from their mothers they picked up from other women. A large proportion were excellent singers and reciters, and some avid and consistent readers. Fewer girls worked their way through college than did boys, but they earned great respect when they did. If there was envy, it was unspoken.

As a rule our girls married the first year after graduation from high school. There were no wedding trips; they settled in at once as full-fledged ranch wives. The dominant impression our girls made was one of honesty, competence, and a good heart. They were not only able but were willing and ready to be future wives and mothers of the next generation in our valley. There was hardly a girl who, by the second year in high school, was not able to manage a household. Not one of us boys would have been ready to found and maintain a home.

Generally we children in school held our serious discussions in winter around the red-hot stove at lunch time. In good weather we would be busy outdoors with baseball and other games. The girls, most days, herded off by themselves, but sometimes joined in our arguments. Two girls were intellectually and in sheer beauty superior to all others, although a number were remarkable youngsters. One was a daughter of a German family, Dunkards, pious, energetic, and skillful ranchers. Women and girls of this persuasion dressed in plain habits of sober colors, wearing close-fitting bonnets tied under the chin, with a border of ruffled white cambric or lace. This girl was tall, with the proportions of a Juno, a model for any sculptor, with bright blue eyes and flaxen hair, a lovely Gretchen straight out of Saxony. The other girl, a brunette, was from a Quaker family. She was of medium height, with a porcelain complexion, a Tanagra figure, grave brown eyes and exquisite profile. They were a handsome pair. Whenever girls joined us in debate we all listened to these two. All the sincerity and depth of religious backgrounds shone in their faces and echoed in voice and ideas.

One cold day as we were clustered about the potbellied

stove, talk ranged over many subjects—work on the Panama Canal, the exploits of Senator Borah, conservation, and, probably due to the presence of our two most spiritually-minded girls, without effort on their part, it finally concentrated on religious subjects.

One boy, clever in argument, posed the question of the problem of suffering. The Dunkard girl, in her lovely voice, never raised in vehemence, made a good case that most suffering was self-caused, but left room for the mysterious and senseless side of history covering such categorics as the pain of innocent children and inherited disabilities. In this connection she mentioned frankly a blind child we all knew whose affliction was due to venereal disease on the part of his parents.

Talk went around, finally arriving at the problem of forgiveness for wrong done. The Quaker girl, gentle, clear-eyed and clearheaded, became our leader. She pointed out that forgiveness was, to be sure, a religious obligation if we were to take the Lord's Prayer seriously, but she pressed hard for forgiveness as a practical matter to relieve us of ruinous emotions which blemished the lives of so many of our parents. "It's one of the few things which will make you free," she said. "Free inside." She pointed out that, with each one of us life centered about some hot spot, good ones such as love of land, patriotism, animals, skills, family reputation, or bad ones, such as hatred, vengeance or egotism.

As we listened to these beautiful, devout girls we knew they had the word. The long, venomous duel with my stepmother made me aware of the need for some mutual forgiveness on our ranch. Something had to break, or give.

Like adolescents anywhere, among the boys there was a strong interest in sex. Life among the animals did take away what in city boys might have been unsatisfied curiosity. The facts were obvious for all to see. It is fair to say that we had a fierce protectiveness regarding our girl schoolmates. Whatever directions a boy's amorous thoughts or inclinations might take, there was a solid wall of feeling against anyone who would have imposed upon our girls. There may have been some lovemaking, but, if so, it was very secret.

Over in Ontario, Oregon, some fifteen miles away, there was a whorehouse but none of us would ever have been allowed in it. There was also a famous Alley in Boise, a town few of us ever saw. The going price was one dollar. Most of the boys were kept from promiscuity by sheer timidity before the mystery of sex, by religious convictions, however dimly felt, or fear of venereal disease, and a desire to play fair with the girls—all sound enough reasons.

Most kids in Idaho did not ride to school on burros or horses as many had done at Dry Gulch School on Minnesota Creek in Colorado. Nearly all of us walked, joining up along the roads, and we had much fun, often eating noonday lunches before reaching school. In spring the perfume of orchards was everywhere, and one small field we passed was always planted in turnips, beautiful they were, the size of crab apples, white, with a purple blush, sweet and cool and delicious to the tongue. One little girl had a pinto pony, a painted pony as we called it, named Calico, with big spots of black on his white hide. Some teachers had fine horses which they housed in a small livery stable during the day. These were ridden back and forth to ranches where their owners boarded. Women teachers were as able riders as the men.

In addition to baseball and pullaway at school, our games included horseshoe pitching. There were always plenty of horseshoes about. Little went on in the few stores on most days. The clerks would be out pitching horseshoes. Their shouts of triumph on a lucky throw would cause us kids to giggle and interrupt our lessons.

We boys did all we could to hasten the day we would reach man's estate. As many children are, I was fearful of the dark. Some anxieties are never confessed to anyone, at least at the time. We did have a strong tradition to surmount bodily weaknesses, to achieve physical prowess. A milestone toward becoming a man was passed when we were able to pitch large shocks of alfalfa onto hayracks in stacking time, to be admitted as an equal member to the working crew of the men. A fierce, competitive spirit urged us to become good horsemen, drivers, irrigators, baseball players, marksmen, horseshoers, and mechanics. But we concealed an ambition to overcome our inner handicaps to conquer the fears which were our secrets, and we never discussed them.

To become tough and hard we would sleep on the floor or out in the open, go without food and water for a day and a night, walk miles into the brush with heavy pack, and other self-imposed stunts. Often, to defeat fear of the dark, when older ones were sound asleep, I would go to the corrals. Horses, mules, cows, colts, and calves would crowd around, giving recognition and courage. On blackest nights it was easy to tell what animal was near. Colts and calves, inquisitive and friendly, would come to smell and to rub noses against me. Darkness and light were the same to them.

I made myself take long walks in the darkness, listening to squirrels and rabbits scurrying about their business, and to the pleasant sounds of water running over low weirs in irrigation ditches. South, at a short distance was the main canal, wide and deep, bringing the wealth of the Payette River to the thirsty valley, with now and then a water rat or a fish splashing in the flood. No matter how black the night, the silhouette of the height of land toward the Snake River Valley stood out sharply against the sky, permanent, reassuring.

Riding long distances at night also helped overcome childish timidity. One could think and plan, and in this be assisted by conversation with the horse whose sensitive and mobile ears evidenced sharp attention to all being said. The condition and atmosphere along the road were an exact indication of the season. In spring new grass gave off its own smells. Passing orchards in bloom one could tell which nearby blooming trees were peach, or apple, or pear, or plum. In high summer alfalfa under water could easily be detected, the road dust had its own odors, differing as the terrain changed its nature from mile to mile, and, in harvest time no smell is sweeter than drying hay recently cut. In autumn on blackest nights one knew when he was passing a ranch house, for the sharp ammonia reek of stables, corrals and manure piles could tell man and horse where they were, for each ranch had a different smell. The soft swish and gurgle of irrigation ditches crossing the roads would often cause one to dismount and give drink to horse and self. When winter storms swept the land, riders wrapped faces in old mufflers, put newspapers front and back beneath coats and trusted our horses to find the way. Rises and falls along familiar roads gave an indication of distances, and a horse never mistakes his own turning toward home and feed and shelter. Gradually acute fear of the dark passed away.

Boys on the sagebrush flats were greatly interested in exploits of Peary in his dashes for the North Pole. When Dr. Frederick A. Cook claimed that he had reached the Pole we divided up about fifty-fifty. There were curses, high words, and fistfights. These were exciting times for Americans were learning to fly—Barrian, the Wrights, Curtiss, Moissant, and others.

Sunday nights, chores done, we teen-agers sometimes gathered in a home where there was an organ. We sang school songs and hymns, and often played kissing games such as Post Office. One person chosen to start would be put in a closed room. He or she would send out word that there was a postcard or a letter, for so-and-so. There were no packages, for parcel post was not yet inaugurated. Parcels in those days were sent by Adams, American, or Wells, Fargo Express to railroad stations where the operator was freight agent, ticket seller, telegrapher, and also handler of parcels.

A postcard in our kissing games mean a simple handshake. Then this person who had been called in was allowed to send out a notice in his or her turn. A letter meant a hug and a kiss. Let no one think lewdly—no bad consequences came from our simple rural pleasures!

Almost every summer there were forest fires in Montana, Idaho, Oregon, and Washington. Timberlands were being ruthlessly exploited in these years. It is encouraging today to see how firmly the notion of conservation of land, forest, and wildlife is taking hold. It was not only due to carelessness upon the part of lumbermen that we had such destructive forest fires, but also to lightning and to sparks from locomotives. Hardly a summer passed that we did not have the sun almost hidden by a blue haze of smoke from fires sometimes hundreds of miles away. The most destructive conflagration in western history was the Tillamook fire which swept from west of Portland, Oregon, to the coast, an inferno which destroyed millions of wildlife and vast fortunes in trees. This was superbly written up by a man with my name, in a book entitled *Fire.*

One of the most pathetic occurrences in a country community is an auction of household goods. Of course it is a quick and efficient way to liquidate an estate, large or small, but it is especially sad when it is the final scene in what is most often a tragedy. When a family moved out of the area, or the old folks died, went broke, or just gave up, then the bills would go up announcing an auction. It hurt to see greedy buyers bidding in plows, horses, cows, other livestock, and furniture, for peanuts, which had been come by with such toil and privation. Auctioneers always had their little jokes about chamber pots and such-like family possessions. These jokes were the same at each auction but always brought guffaws from the men, as women hid smiles under their sunbonnets.

What really hurt was to see weapons, which we boys would have walked a hundred miles to own, go for a dollar or two. Then, also, there were exquisite quilts with hundreds of pieces of colored cloth, and thousands of stitches, never used. One old maid died who had made two quilts, worthy of a museum, for her wedding bed, but her betrothed had been killed at Shiloh. She never married.

My stepmother shed a few tears that night as we talked over the auction for the quilts had been bid in by a rapacious old woman for two dollars each. I never liked country auctions.

Once a number of automobiles came through our valley on the abominable roads. They were on some sort of transcontinental race or test. Our Doctor Drisdale who cared for the whole valley, purchased a Buick. It was light gray, buttoned up behind, had two seats and seemed to me the most beautiful thing I had ever seen. One day he came by on his way to a patient near Falk's Store some ten miles to the east. He asked me if I would like a ride. He needed to ask only once—it was heavenly. But for work on the ranches only horses were employed. I never saw a tractor until years later.

Swapping, hiring, working out on other ranches, buying and selling, taught some built-in facts of life. In black moments, when I had been cheated in some deal, perhaps paltry but important to me, due to my own stupidity or the meanness of others, there occurred periods of discouragement. It seemed at these times that life was an eternal combat and that if it were ever true that the meek should inherit the earth, it nevertheless appeared that liars, thieves, and bullies would soon repossess it. The devil-take-the-hindmost seemed to cover a lot of human behavior. The fool and his money, or land, or animals, soon parted—that was clear. But I could not deny that friendship, trust, kindness, and love were also solid facts. These outweighed for me the evil traits in the human heart.

Our teachers insisted on the twin ideals of private excellence and public service. Experience and reflection showed both ideals were tenable. I came to measure character in others by a willingness to tell the truth even when it hurt, to attempt to make restitution for wrongdoing, and to measure public service by whether a neighbor lent a hand in any common effort in our valley.

There was nothing softheaded about personal excellence and public service. Somewhere along the line in our schooling a teacher had referred to a soldier, saying, "Put your faith in God, but keep your powder dry." There was no conflict. Sheer ignorance, blind belief that all men were good, and equal, could lead to the destruction of hard-working people, and to the tyranny of the weaker brother. Also, refusal to bear one's share of the common burden could make a desert out of any countryside.

From hot and earnest schoolboy discussion many of us learned that basic conflict in man was not between idealism and realism, nor between science and religion, but between a critical idealism and sheer greed—materialism. We did not live by our convictions, but we did see the truth.

Once a recruiter for immigration to New Zealand spoke in our Opera House about the scenic wonder, the people, the future, and the socialism of his land. We boys and girls were thrilled, and most were ready to go Down Under immediately. The speaker left a ferment in our minds; our discussions continued for weeks. By and large our conclusion was that although it appeared good for the State to own more, and for the individual farmer to own less, it was more just to give the individual large liberty to go as far as his abilities would carry him, and to let the State have well defined regulatory powers. We were capitalists, without much capital, but without apology. We did, without exception, welcome the police power of the State to stop aggressors dead in their tracks, rich and poor alike.

One kid who had a hard time keeping up with the class summed up his impression of our lengthy debate by saying, "You know, I was nearly sent back a grade last year. I guess I am not as smart as some of you. I'll share most of what I have with you—but not everything. I won't give any of you five points off my grades and I won't ask it of you. Each of us has some jobs he must do alone, and he has a right to keep most of what he earns, provided he doesn't hurt anyone else. I am not a socialist. I don't believe in taking from you what I have not sweated for, nor for you taking from me what you have not earned." That about added up our schoolmates' thoughts about the paradise of New Zealand as well as our concept about private excellence and public service and citizenship.

One stormy night Father rode in late from a school board meeting. I always cared for his horse and as I took the reins and began to loose the saddle girths he said, "Son, a friend of yours," and he mentioned a minister, "is in serious trouble. I advise you to avoid talk and to stand by him now, as he will need his friends." He said no more but made his way for the house. Father had never in any way discussed religion or church with me. We never mentioned the matter again, but I deeply appreciated his attitude, he had honor and expected it of me, and honor had no reprieve, no statute of limitations in his book.

Nearly every fruit-growing valley has a cider mill to use up the produce not good enough to ship. One Sunday afternoon in late autumn some of us boys took a hike across country to such a mill where we purchased a gallon of cider. It was cold, sparkling, and very hard. I drank a fair amount, made my way home toward nightfall and, after feeding the stock, found I was drunk as a tick. I lay down on the haystack and fell into a drugged sleep. Long after dark my father came out to see what was going on. Finding me asleep and soaked, for it had been raining, he roused me and I explained what had happened. "Don't do it again," was all he said. Was I sick! Father went on the principle that nearly all big things can be reduced to little things and most little things to nothing.

Hiring out for short periods, when our work permitted, not only brought in a little useful hard money, but gave a wider knowledge of humanity. Some miles to the east was a point called Falk's Store, a very old settlement on one of the many shortcuts on the old Oregon Trail. No one of us knew who founded it, or when.

Falk's Store and an adjacent ranch of several hundred acres were owned by an old bachelor, a tough hombre who had a bad reputation, and deserved it. The store building itself was a patched-up tumbled-down shack, unpainted, with big hitching poles in front, bolted onto cottonwood posts. Illegal whiskey, some hardware, various staples, tobacco, leather-mending material, shirts, overalls, and some canned goods were sold.

The bottomland consisted of patches of wild hay, small fields of alfalfa, alternating with desolate alkali flats, not a pleasant place. On this ran a herd of nondescript cattle. The dwelling house was a boar's nest, the owner living alone most of the time. Occasionally he persuaded some poor couple to house there, with the wife doing the cooking. There were five or six rooms full of stuff collected over decades. Broken jugs and dishes, cans, buckets, harness and saddles, old ropes, clothing, bottles, furniture with the stuffing breaking out, old papers and magazines, smelly horse blankets, rusty tools and varied debris covered the floor, bound together with cobwebs. Windows had perhaps never been washed; they were covered with flyspecks. There were a few broken panes over which cardboard had been nailed.

Once I helped him hay—two dollars and a half a day, man, team, and wagon, for ten hours in the field. That year he had secured a couple newly come from England. Both were splendid people, small, neat, timid, and eager to please. The woman prepared meals for us; the man helped in the haying. The wife made a big effort to clean up the mess, to wash windows, and to organize the kitchen.

It happened that the rancher had with him a giant nephew who had ridden up cross-country from a ranch where he had been cowpunching in Nevada. This nephew was a hairy ape, a loudmouthed, foul, illiterate, brutal, drunken woman chaser, a type utterly without humane or moral qualities. He followed the poor English woman about as unabashed as a rutting stag, insulting her husband, and clutching at the wife in the presence of us all. The uncle seemed amused at the behavior of his uncouth nephew.

On the second day of haying, while the brute was pitching shocks of alfalfa onto the Englishman's wagon, he suddenly flew into a frenzy of cursing and began beating the stranger with the flat of his pitchfork. By the time I drove up, the Englishman was lying on his back in his wagon, unconscious and covered with blood. I took him to the house where I helped the wife wash and bandage him. The nephew roared about the place threatening bloody murder. Both man and wife were terror stricken, without protection, broke, in a foreign land, with no friends, unable to stand up for themselves against such savages.

That night as I prepared to leave, the rancher asked if I would help finish the haying. I declined. Going home I had a heavy heart for these innocent strangers. Never having been a real part of our scattered community, the owner had a hard time after that securing any help. The couple moved away when the husband recovered—where, I do not know.

The village of New Plymouth had little to offer of beauty or interest. We bought our provisions in the few stores, but the center of our lives was the ranches, none well developed as yet. Our entire existence revolved around soil, school, irrigation, our animals, and our people. There was one spot, however, that did have drama, the blacksmith's shop. The blacksmith was an ungainly fellow, necessarily very strong to shoe reluctant or even savage horses, to mend broken farm equipment, and even to build entire wagons.

The glow of his fire, the wheeze of the bellows which we were allowed to pump when we brought work to be done, the rhythm of his hammer sounding dully on red-hot iron, ringing like music when the hammer slid off onto the anvil, made a good day for us boys. Like most smiths he had a regular sequence of five blows upon the iron, then over to the anvil, where the hammer bounced and sang for about the space of two blows, as he examined his work, striking each sequence a little harder as the red iron, cooled to orange and then to black, became more resistant.

We felt it was a special privilege to help on many jobs, preparing hoofs of horses and mules for shoeing, drilling holes in strap iron, and even simple welding. We brought in carefully saved pieces of iron when we needed repairs, for only seldom did he have new stock. For strap metal old wagon tires were excellent, mattering little what gauge or width they were. We were not seeking beauty, but utility. Some boys acquired genuine skill in tasks about the shop.

Summer was hard on wheels, for wagons stood in the weather the entire year. Along our road were no barns to house farm equipment; only crude sheds to protect animals. In cold months horses and cows ran loose in corrals or fields to find shelter as they could. To tie up a horse or cow in temperatures far below zero could easily cost the life of a valuable animal.

The felloes of wagon wheels, that is, the wooden rim into which the spokes were fitted, shrank badly in intense summer heat, necessitating a tighting of the iron tires, a job requiring skill.

The blacksmith followed an exact and unchanging routine. First he took off the loose tire, then cleaned the felloes, repairing any damaged section or broken spoke with odd pieces of maple, oak, or hickory left over from other jobs. Next he heated about a foot of the tire red hot and placed the tire around the felloes. Then, quickly, using a device with a long handle, to give him leverage, he shrank the tire to the felloes. It sounds easy—but try it!

In contact with the hot iron, the felloes would smoke and even burst into flame. At this point the smith doused the whole wheel in water. This done, the iron tire fitted tightly. To prevent loosening of these iron tires we frequently ran wagons into irrigation ditches to swell the felloes.

The blacksmith, who was almost illiterate and very rough, was by far the best mechanic in our section. He knew the name of every workhorse, mule, or child for miles around, and taught us many tricks. We were always treated kindly in the shop; he showed us respect and affection, and we paid him back in his own coin.

Barbershops out there all had a tin tub with some arrangement for heating water, generally a kerosene lamp. Haircuts were twenty-five cents, a bath a half a dollar.

Sheepherders would come in from a winter with bands of sheep in remote places, for a general cleanup, covered with beard to the eyes, with hair over their shoulders. After the barber had trimmed them they would soak in the tub until the water was cold. When dressed in clean clothing they would be unrecognizable.

A new crop was being introduced into the Payette Valley—sugar beets. It took some years before problems of planting, thinning, harvesting, and marketing could be sorted out. Our family never went in for beets. The thinning was done by Japanese crews, secured for the ranchers through a sugar factory over in the Snake River Valley. Japanese workers seemed to like the stoop labor. They were quick and skillful, and hard drinkers. They brought bottled beer to the fields in gunnysacks, left it in the sun, to drink warm. I never saw a Japanese drunk, but they put away enormous quantities. In one month their bar bill at Klaus Peter's saloon in Payette was twelve hundred dollars. They were friendly with us children, showing us photographs of their families back in Japan, and exchanging words.

A local telephone company was organized which had a party line connecting ranches along our road. The drugstore owner, his wife and two daughters were the principal operators. There was much listening in on one another's conversations and no one minded. Often talk went on with four or five neighbors at the same time. It broke up the loneliness for many ranchers' wives.

Our country operators were an extraordinary group of women. There were no ungracious ones. Any hour of the day or night you were pretty sure to find from them desired information, who was expecting, the location of the doctor, that such a one was at the village having his horses shod, that a boy had enlisted in the Marines, that a neighbor woman was picking strawberries and would not be in her house until noon. These wonderful women operators were the gazetteers of the whole valley; they bound us together, seemingly humiliated if they did not have on tap the item wanted. Often a woman on a lonely homestead would call in to Central just for a chat, even men did that.

Why, I do not know, but on cold nights with the temperature ten, fifteen, or twenty-five degrees below zero these lines would suddenly begin to hum and sing, and as suddenly stop. When this noise began one knew it was cold.

Hardly ever did I go over three or four miles from our ranch. But once we needed two thousand board feet of unplaned sheathing lumber. Another rancher joined us in the effort to go to a lumber mill in the mountains beyond Emmett to the east, up near Squaw Butte, to help bring a load. We planned to double up the teams on tough hills. Food for ourselves and the horses was packed in the wagons. We went up the Payette Valley for some twenty-five miles before the road began to climb. Suddenly, ahead of us, lay the most formidable part of the route, Picket Corral Hill. As we approached I could hardly believe my eyes! As if painted on the steep hillside in ten sharp zigzags and hairpin turns the white road from a distance seemed almost straight up and down. My anxiety was in some manner communicated to the horses. The neighbor and his team ahead seemed to be gripped by the same fear. Could we make it up the hill empty, let alone come down without the heavily laden wagons overrunning our splendid horses? Could we negotiate the hairpin turns?

We made it up finally, found the mill, and loaded two thousand board feet each. We curried our horses, watered and fed them, ate, and lay down to attempt to sleep. I may have slept some, but in the mind of each of us drivers, and I am sure in the horses' minds, was the dreaded Picket Corral Hill. Next morning we stopped on arrival at the descent, chained our back wheels so they could not turn, cut saplings, arranging them as additional drag brakes, and crept down the hill, stage by stage, to each turning. The horses were as fearful as were we, but in a strange manner both horses and drivers seemed to feel we must not panic; we had to get through this experience. With wildly rolling eyes every horse, nevertheless, kept steady, though trembling. Late that night, on arriving home, I went into our kitchen to wash up and have a bite. I looked in the mirror to see if I was white haired!

By far the best times we children had in winter were when we skated on a big pond caused by backwater from a dike on the irrigation canal and covering many acres. Late Saturdays we would come there to skate when wood chopping was over. At night big fires of sagebrush would be lighted. Under starlit skies with the frost below zero and the ice booming in the cold we had some of the most memorable hours life shall give.

In 1907 a bank failed in a city far away from us but it thrust the iron of poverty deep into the soul of our valley. The Knickerbocker Trust Company in New York City closed its doors. There were columns about it in the Spokane *Spokesman-Review*, but few of us thought such distant occurrences would touch our lives. There was the usual accompaniment of ruined banks, bankrupt companies, men jumping out of hotel windows, scandal, and recrimination. The East recovered in a few months, but the money illness remained a long time in our section of the West where there was little capital. For nearly a year we were without real money. Clearinghouse certificates were employed until they were worn to bits. We sold the best first cutting alfalfa, in prime condition, for four dollars per ton in the stack. No one talked much about it for we were used to hard times. A good man could be hired for twenty dollars per month that year in the summer season, and many were willing to work in the winter for board alone.

The history of thousands of western ranches is a story of three or four failures and a final success. A man starves and slaves to prove up on a claim, that is, reside upon it and make necessary improvements to satisfy the government. He then sells out, or is forced to leave before he can reap the fruits of his sweat and toil. Then another, and another, invests the savings he has brought from Nebraska or Iowa or Pennsylvania. After several abandon or sell at a sacrifice, someone buys the land at a reasonable price, reaping benefits of his predecessors' failures. He then is able to make a living.

The usual cycle of ascending prices, broken fortunes, and frustrated hopes, until fictitious values were adjusted to the actual capacity of the land to produce and the market to absorb, was experienced both in Idaho and in Colorado. Boom psychology is as native to the West as whiskey, corn bread and bacon.

Across the Snake River to the west lay the immense area of southern and central Oregon, without a railway clear over to Klamath Lake where the Shasta Route went down from Portland to San Francisco. From Payette, Idaho, and Ontario, Oregon, there still went west into this country the last of the big freight wagons with as many as twenty horses or mules pulling them. Drivers were not only skilled horsemen but were also good horseshoers and blacksmiths, for brakes, harness, and wheels needed constant repairs. Almost daily some animal would fling a shoe, or a wagon break down. We boys studied every detail of these wagons with their oversize wheels, watching tricks of different drivers as they handled horses. Most drivers used a single line as it was impossible to employ reins for so many horses. The greatest hazard was for leaders to jackknife—to turn back, on a difficult road. It was a sight to see a string of laboring horses drawing a wagon laded with tons of merchandise, dust almost obscuring the ones in front, the driver high up on his seat with a handkerchief tied below his eyes to allow him to breathe. Roads were hardly more than trails.

Sheep raising was important in our county. Throughout southern Idaho lava deserts and forested mountain ranges alternated with alfalfa and fruit districts. Great expanses of sagebrush make a favorable land for sheep. Government Reserves in the mountains were within easy access, providing unparalleled summer pasture. Canyon County, where we lived, had over two million sheep.

One winter, my fourth year of high school, which I did not attend, doing my studies at home, I helped tend a band of twenty-five hundred sheep, with a Scotchman named

Henderson and a Basque named Jesus Manuel Aryata. The cold often reached thirty below zero. We slept with our clothes on in a tent with dogs at the foot of our blankets to keep us warm. Horses we turned loose to keep them from freezing. We had our food and thirty dollars a month pay. Those dollars were big, as big as an acre covered with snow! A camp tender came around once every two weeks to leave us food. The Scotchman drank gallons of Lipton tea laced with whiskey. After the men were in their blankets and asleep I would put two lanterns on a box beside me and study algebra, plane and solid geometry, English, a book course in physics, and Cicero's *Orations.* Nothing could have been a better training for concentrated study. As this was my last year of high school, every two months I went to New Plymouth to take examinations in order to graduate in the spring.

On the few Sundays of the summer when we did not work it was an exciting relief to slip into tall sagebrush beyond the settled country, there to dream of lands across the mountains and to watch wild desert life. On first appearance there seem to be few animals and no vegetable life save the sage; but when one lies still and watches there is a teeming world of busy insects and animals, and scores of plant forms. Many varieties of ants thrive in the brush, great red ones half an inch long, which build nests as large as bushel baskets from small sticks, bark, and sand grains. There are white ants, black ants, ladybugs with red backs spotted with black, many spiders and millions of grass-hoppers. Field mice abounded and short-tailed ground squirrels, which next to the jackrabbits, were the greatest pest of the ranchers. These squirrels made subterranean passages which were the despair of the irrigator. The first task in putting a new field under irrigation was to drown out these rodents and destroy their tunnels. Dogs would kill them until they were weary. Water would follow these underground channels and throw the irrigation plan awry. There were also birds in the brush, magpies, an occasional crow, small owls and tiny sparrow-like creatures. Now and then a mile overhead were V-shaped squadrons of sandhill cranes, their legs dragging grotesquely behind, circling down upon small marshes along the big irrigation ditch lined with brown-headed tules or cattails. Meadowlarks and rabbits cleverly took evasive action to protect their young. They flopped about pretending to be wounded.

Country children are fortunate in being closer to nature than those who live in cities. They lack comforts of town dwellers but have many compensations. On the journey to Colorado from Idaho, which I made several times, the route passes vast shallow swamps where the Bear River flowing south below Pocatello empties into Great Salt Lake. In those days were sights seldom encountered any other place on earth; millions of ducks and geese in the area almost blotted out the sun. Among them were other aquatic birds and waders of several species. Years later I discussed this astonishing phenomenon with Dr. Hornaday, head of the Bronx Zoo, the famous author of *The Mind and Manners of Wild Animals.* Familiar with the Bear River region, he told me that water from this stream had been increasingly diverted to irrigation. This caused the large expanse of water at the mouth of the Bear, only inches deep, to become increasingly alkaline and poisonous, killing countless waterfowl. Government people cleverly solved the problem by throwing up miles of low barrages which held fresh water from the river and the snow and rain, resulting in dilution of excessively saline swamps until the situation was again acceptable to ducks, geese, and other visitors. We did not have much accurate knowledge of the wildlife about us but we were deeply interested in fur and fin and feather.

Desert growth presents fascinating variations. In summer early morning there are pink primroses, delicate and fragile as orchids, which melt under the first blast of the sun, several sorts of aromatic sage, chico, skunkbrush, wild onions, minute fungi and lichen which nestle at the foot of the sage, small cacti with rich red and yellow blossoms, and many sorts of grasses. One boy in the valley, Francis Mc-

Bride, came to know much of the flora of this region. Over a score of species, which he was the first to classify, bear his name. He was called to the Gray Herbarium at Harvard University and became a leading authority on the plant life of the arid West. He later served in Copenhagen and various other botanical research centers. Lying on my back in the sand hills on hot Sunday afternoons I received my first lessons in the structure of plants and animals.

Each autumn I worked for Francis McBride's father, a retired doctor from Iowa who had planted an orchard near New Plymouth. I would stay until the apple harvest was over, returning in the spring to help with spraying. We used arsenate of lead to spray the bloom as a protection against the coddling moth, the usual source of apple worms. Also a vile, stinking mixture of sulphur and lime was employed to kill the San José scale. The damnable stuff was capable of blinding a man. In fact the bursting of a hose often caused serious accidents. The McBrides meant a lot to me; father, mother, and son were widely read and often loaned me books.

Any community is lucky to have one family which will take full social responsibility and assume leadership for the common good. In the Payette Valley we had such a family. Comyn S. French came from Vermont originally. He was our local banker and one-time state senator. He and his son Fred and their wives organized a Sunday school in their home, near our ranch, some four miles from New Plymouth.

We needed a local school for little children, as it was downright dangerous in winter for small boys and girls to attempt the long walk to the village in sub-zero cold. At a community meet in the French home it was decided that we would build a schoolhouse ourselves. Each rancher gave what he could, paint, nails, brick, lumber, shingles, or work. My father gave the roof. Occasionally we had preaching there, and Christmas parties for the children. Then came a local chapter of the Grange and Farmers' Institutes. The intense individualism of the human beavers in the valley was mellowed by the example of our finest families giving themselves in public service. I learned from the French family the meaning of *noblesse oblige.* Many times they must have been discouraged, but they never showed it.

At the Valley View school we had gatherings to discuss ranch problems. Several times my stepmother was chosen to give papers on chicken and turkey raising, cooking and gardening. Composed with clarity, organization, and practical knowledge, in her copperplate handwriting, and delivered in the same lovely voice with which she read books to Father, me, and the hired men, the talks were a revelation to half-literate farmers and wives, clustered about the stove in the schoolhouse. In later years these meetings were followed by more extensive and equally fruitful discussions by agricultural people from the state and county.

All winters were severe, but one was positively ferocious. It was impossible to accumulate sagebrush fuel for any considerable period in advance, as it burned up so quickly. When a series of almost continuous snowstorms overtook us, it was necessary for me to go up into the waste above the big irrigation ditch in the midst of the whisper and hissing of the white downpour, to bring in a load. I would often come across other boys or men on the same errand. Storms were often so heavy that those gathering fuel could not see one another until very close. Horses, however, would always be aware that someone was about, restlessly exchanging whinnies. We all allowed our teams to find their way home on their own through sand washes and arroyos, for we could not possibly have guided them, and they never erred. Another source of fuel was prunings from the orchards. Small branches, which would have been scorned in a region of ample fuel, were for us very precious.

On a night full of wind and sleet I had a painful accident. Near our outdoor privy was a pile of planks, one of which had a few rusty spikes sticking through it. We were careful about such hazards on account of horses as well as human beings, but one plank had been missed. With the thermometer well below zero on this night I felt the call of nature. Strong winds pushed me out of the path and I stepped squarely on a rusty spike, drove it through a heavy shoe and deeply into my foot. Yells for my father to rescue me could not be heard above the howling of the blast. By sheer accident he came out the door, saw me crawling toward the house, dragging the plank. He pulled the plank and spike away and carried me into the kitchen. I cannot describe the pain. A clean rifle bullet is pleasant in comparison. No doctor was available, so my father and stepmother applied the old country remedy to prevent lockjaw, or tetanus. They washed my foot in water as hot as I could stand, then bandaged on some salt pork. This application was changed twice a day for a week. A puncture is harder to treat than a cut.

My stepmother's skill with chickens, guineas and turkeys was unusual. Guineas are handsome, exotic, and can easily be a nuisance. We generally had a few in lieu of watchdogs. The slightest distraction or unfamiliar incident triggers off a tremendous racket. If geese saved Rome, certainly guineas sounding the alarm have saved many ranches from raids by hawks and coyotes.

One year, with only two turkey hens and a gobbler my stepmother made a handsome profit, taking eggs from under turkey hens each day to prevent them from setting, and placing them under chicken hens, a common practice on the ranches. From the eggs from her two turkey hens she raised enough birds to realize over one hundred dollars, and in addition we had several, to eat ourselves. Not only was she a superb cook, wrote exquisitely, but was a fine manager of all affairs within her control. I fully recognized her great qualities. However, although we were mutually dependent in those years, we were totally hostile to each other.

In most newly settled regions thoughtful and energetic ranchers experiment with various strains and breeds of animals and fowls until they discover those which best meet their needs. Thus my stepmother tried out several kinds of chickens to determine which combined the maximum weight with the longest laying periods. Red and White Leghorns, Wyandottes, Rhode Island Reds, Black Minorcas, Buff Orpingtons and others were tested. She finally chose Plymouth Rocks. She knew every hen; many were named. Hens have a peculiar behavior when they have decided to set and to raise a family of chicks. To discourage this, to "break up" the setting process, as ranchers call it, she would persist in lifting hens off their nests, allowing only chosen ones to hatch the eggs which kept a larger number laying. When eggs hatched under the setting hens she made large shallow pans of corn bread, which she crumbled up, much relished by the chicks. She was the only person I knew who could induce sympathetic personality traits in chickens! Hens with chicks who would fly at me in a fury of pecking, responded quietly to her gentleness and understanding of their needs. Neighbors were loud in praise of astonishing results which were achieved.

Ducks and geese we never raised as they played about too much in irrigation ditches, disturbing the set of water in the fields.

The tension between my stepmother and me increased during these especially frigid months. On any basis she was a remarkable woman. Always she was immaculate in her person and kept the house so, as far as possible under adverse conditions.

One night, with the temperature below zero, I came in, long after dark, from feeding the stock. I had been out all day pulling alfalfa out of a stack, loading it onto a hayrack to feed sheep. There had been a long series of killer storms, we had been working long hours, money was scarce and all three of us were on edge. We saw almost no one, worked day after day without much talk. At night we slept in icy rooms with no heat, we were ground down, it was a low moment.

After taking off my boots I asked if I might have something to eat, for the two had long since finished their supper. She, probably exhausted by fatigue and worry, turned about and struck me in the face. Something snapped in my brain.

"Goddam you, I'll kill you!" I shouted.

My father separated us. I went into my room, without eating, to struggle with my hatred, my remorse, and the cold, until the alarm clock sounded at four-thirty in the morning, the time to go to the corrals to begin another day. No word was said of the row of the previous night. We were on the bottom. When my father rode off early next morning, while it was still black night, he said briefly "Son, we shall get out of this. This is the year we must bite the bullet!"

Eventually my stepmother and I came to love each other, made up for years of savage strife. As a grown man, on Mother's Day I always tried to say a good word for stepmothers. It is one thing to care for one's own children, it is another to rear and love another's boy or girl.

At the close of that terrible winter, although first-cutting hay in September in the stack had sold for four and a half to five dollars a ton, in late January, February, and March it had risen to thirty and even forty dollars a ton. A number of rather shady characters, although it was in truth a legitimate business operation, jumped into the market to buy up everything in sight, for they knew sheep barons would pay rather than let valuable bands starve.

At this time my father and stepmother went to Colorado leaving me in full charge of everything. He was attempting to salvage as much as possible from his former holdings.

We were in the fortunate position of having more than enough good hay to see us through until first cutting. I therefore let a number of neighbors, who were short, borrow to meet their needs. They agreed to return an equal value at harvest, but I expressly stipulated the value was not to be calculated at the highly inflated rate. It was fair enough to receive in actual measure more than I had loaned, under these circumstances, but I did not want to gouge. Every neighbor, save one, paid me back more than fairly.

There was, however, one new rancher, really a stranger,

who in late February was hard pressed for feed. I let him have all he needed until first cutting of hay in July, on the same deal as with the others. When time came to repay, the new man brought back less than he borrowed, green stuff, of poor grade, full of weeds, without reference to the better dry hay I loaned him when he was in a jam, claiming he had repaid me in full, all this, with much profanity. He had received over one hundred fifty dollars value, he returned a twenty dollar value. It gave me a shock. All our neighbors were tough but scrupulous with one another on all matters, except horse trading, which was understood. Aunt Margaret used to say, "People are like horses, some good, some bastards. You don't know until you deal with 'em. Some are just plain shits—it's a matter of breed." I took the abuse, for this bruiser was twice as big as I, with hard fists the size of hams. He soon sold and moved away and no one missed him; he was not one of ours.

A preacher held some special meetings in the Opera House at New Plymouth during that year. This was the building used by the medicine merchants, for dances, for Farmers' Institutes and public gatherings. I went to these services out of curiosity; the direct preaching of the evangelist made a powerful appeal. I felt keenly the difference between what I was and what I ought to be. I had the sort of conversion described by William James in his *The Varieties of Religious Experience,* simple and profound.

That night as I rode home the Northern Lights were blazing, the Milky Way a great white banner across the sky. My horse seemed different—so did ranches I passed, and Squaw Butte on the eastern horizon, our own place, all the world. I tried to remember when I should commit my first sin after having repented and been forgiven. Well, I have sinned much since that hour, but the experience will never leave me. I am a believer. This is written with no pride, for who can boast of spiritual prowess? This I know, faith is my most precious possession—I am a believer.

Having set my heart on going to college, and necessarily

eager to lay my hands on money, I fell into a curious manner of achieving this aim. An English emigrant family in some strange manner had come straight from Yorkshire without knowing a single soul in our valley and without any promise of a job. The neighbors rustled around, found a vacant house, and, although they had few things to spare, chairs, tables, beds, blankets, and cooking utensils were brought together. The newcomers were taught how to make do in the winter which that year was severe.

The man, a skilled orchardist, talked to me about grafting roots and how money could be made. All varieties of apples, and there are over two hundred, are achieved by taking the current year's growth of the variety desired, the scions, as they are called, cutting them square across, with at least two or three buds on each piece, taking a wild root, cutting corresponding niches in each, fitting the pieces together, then wrapping the cuts where the two pieces are joined with waxed thread. They are then stored in sand until spring, ready for planting.

How to get the wild seedling roots? It was easy to secure scions. In well pruned orchards in an irrigated region the yearly growth is superb. I could get all the scions I wanted for nothing, cleaning up behind the pruners. I wrote to the Stark Brothers nursery in Missouri who developed the old standbys, the Ben Davis, the Jonathan, the Rome Beauty and the red and yellow Delicious, that I had available about fifty varieties of scions. I also wrote other nurseries from whom favorable answers came back. They could furnish me wild seedling roots, and would buy scions!

Came the roots and the Englishman and I sat up nights in a cellar to do the grafting. It was a beautiful job, and the sale of scions was a bonanza. I realized over three hundred dollars which was a lot of money for me. And I had about one thousand roots grafted with Jonathan and Rome Beauty scions, which I sold for two hundred and seventy-five dollars.

This was the first time I was able to keep for myself money I had earned. It was not that my father demanded money I received on other ranches or that I was being noble in placing my money in the common pot. We were plain up against harsh realities; we would sink or swim together. I had longed for a bike, but had never been able to amass enough money. To hell with a bicycle now, I was going to college!

When left alone to manage the ranch, I began to sell off stock, hay, and generally liquidate our possessions, for Father had decided to dispose of this land and to remain in Colorado. I did my own cooking, washing, and mending, and there was also the year's crop to raise and to sell. The hay crop that summer amounted to over one hundred and fifty tons of alfalfa, without a cent paid out for help. As usual, ranchers traded work around, stacking one man's hay after another. We also loaned each other water, as a large stream, head of water, is much more easily managed than a weak flow. I enjoyed immensely being on my own.

Dreams of college were with me day and night. I bought a small suitcase, big enough to hold my few clothes, gave away books to boys and girls who had been in school with me, paid all bills and still had some four hundred and fifty dollars of my own, as well as a much larger sum for my father. Good homes were found for my cats and dogs.

When the moment to depart arrived a boxcar on the Oregon Short Line was secured. This was loaded with some horses, a lot of farm implements and some odds and ends for the journey down to Colorado. Stout beams were framed in to prevent horses from being thrown upon one another as the train lurched. Neighbor women generously packed a box of food for me, a custom generally followed as a parting gift for a friend. Two barrels of water were placed in the car which could be filled whenever necessary at various water tanks en route. A plentiful supply of baled alfalfa for feed and bedding was laid in. There was a real danger of sparks from the locomotive flying in at the half-open door. A brakeman warned me about this, as recently a circus had had a dreadful accident up near Pendleton, losing twelve horses in a fire caused by sparks. I moved the hay away from the center of the car to the far corner on the engine end, and kept a wet blanket handy.

There was much to remember as the long freight rumbled east and south. The brazen bowl of August skies, black silhouettes of Squaw Butte and the Seven Devils Mountains in early morning, cloud patterns on vast wastes of sagebrush, colors of crops and of plowing on distant ranches, blue haze over everything when forest fires raged in the mountains, greens of willows and cottonwoods along the Payette, the alfalfa when thirsty for water, turning blackish, only to change lush and green when irrigation was laid on; these things we saw and from them we learned.

And the animals—reticence of mules accepting horses' otracism in feeding corrals; the varied temperaments of each; characteristics of the animals as well known to us as those within the family circle, some volatile, nervous, gay, others dull, or choleric; the slightly worried look in faces of raccoons; the unique fidelity of dogs no matter how neglected; the capacity of cats, perhaps best of all mothers, who taught their young to nurse, eat, play, hunt, fight and, finally, to support themselves; the assumed surprise of kittens on meeting one another after a few seconds of separation, spitting and growling, ruffing up their fur in sham hostility. Animals were a near and vivid part of creation in our world.

Nights had their own smells and sounds; always coyotes yapping as near as they dared; tangy musk of polecats; in spring and autumn the honk of geese and ducks on journeys between Canada and Mexico; and always familiar noises of the corrals, the stamping, snorting, feeding, and the rattle of poles as horses and mules rubbed themselves against the fences.

There had been no one in Idaho like Don Meek, our old foreman in Colorado, to disturb or to fertilize our minds by discussion of other than daily occurrences and duties. Our speech and thought had centered on crops, animals, members of the family, mortgages, the black shadow of debt, school, hunting, daily toil on the ranches.

Tragic aspects of life were ignored in our valley or handled with hard, sardonic humor, which is the spiritual armor of frontier people. Whereas Don led us youngsters as far as he could, and that a fair distance, into such queries as, why am I here; what is the chief end of man; what and where is God; how can a just God allow suffering, or untimely death of children, or even of animals; why do good people fail while scoundrels flourish; how do we know what is true and right—of these and of other problems beneath the surface of daily existence—on droughty and reluctant soil of southern Idaho, there was little thought, and no discussion.

To sophisticated observers we were doubtless a dull lot, our ideas lean and restricted. In the first few generations on new land this is inevitable. In early days of New England's settlement handwriting, reading, hymn tunes and every evidence of culture rapidly declined. This process is native to every frontier.

There were wistfulness, ambition, and hunger within these country communities. Like the seeds of some plants which remain dormant for years, until freezing, or even forest fires, enable kernels to burst their hard shells, these hopes slept on, in secret. Second and third generations of pioneers, as struggles for bread and shelter become less severe, managed to found schools and churches and hospitals and universities. Boys and girls of these years who left to work their way through various institutions across the land had a special burden to bear for parents and neighbors often ridiculed book learning, but we boys and girls knew they secretly approved, nevertheless.

The seed, the hunger for knowledge, the thirst for beauty some way persisted until the moment for sprouting arrived. Hopes of somewhat stern and silent ranch men and women were in truth the fruitful seed of immense potentiality, from which, in a more affluent day, led to the establishment of those centers which made possible the flowering of a culture. No frontier heroism shines brighter than that of those church people of various denominations and a few others who, in poverty, established the vast majority of our colleges, universities, hospitals, and schools.

What had kept these ranchers, my friends, going year after year in drought, cold, poverty, hunger, unending work? What lifted their feet and quickened their hands, often when too tired or beaten down to think, going forward with an emotional and spiritual momentum from sheer iron stubbornness? It was promises! Promises were over every aspect of our existence. We seldom discussed them, or even realized them, but they were there, beckoning, reminding, giving courage.

There were promises over uncleared land, promises over newly planted orchards and fields of grain and alfalfa, promises over new houses, better furniture and farm equipment, promises over animals with young, over next year's crops, over children. Looking into a box cradling a new boy baby it was customary for a neighbor to say, "Maybe he'll be President someday!" Mothers would look up with a queer, half-concealed smile. Well, maybe, why not?

There were promises over more adequate schools and local government, and dimly thought out promises about our country, to which we were all devoted without reservation. The drouthy region of Southern Idaho was a land of promises. Yes, in truth, we were broke, but we were never poor.

My big box of food given me by neighbor women was soon exhausted, for I gave away more than I ate to trainmen and hobos. As we thundered along I frequently grew hungry in the boxcar although I had plenty of provisions for the horses. When hungry I thought of food we had had in the valley, for we ate well on the ranches, on most days, but not always! On hungry mornings can any smell equal that of coffee and bacon, with corn bread, thick and moist, with a slab of butter? Or, noonday with fried chicken and new potatoes cooked in a sort of cream sauce? With ham, the women made red-eye gravy, the best on earth, sharp and rich, poured over fried potatoes and hominy grits. And, in season, boiled corn, all one could eat. We had our own honey with the taste of sweet clover, alfalfa, and apple blossoms in it. I tightened my belt, drank lots of water and, in imagination, ate many a good meal, and fed on memories.

On a ranch there are always strong smells: stables and corrals and the animals themselves make up a sort of harmony; the sweated leathers, cleaned and oiled, and sweated once more; and mica axle grease on hot spindles and hubs of loaded wagons. For long periods haystacks went through a fermenting proccss with heat waves coming out the top, giving off a rich odor. And the pleasant smell of guns and powder. We boys had collected pieces of lead pipe and tinfoil, melting them over open fires in cast-off skillets, pouring molten metal into moulds which an old man gave us, to fashion .45-70 slugs we never used, for we had no such rifle. We traded them to men who did. We had, among us, a complete apparatus for making shotgun and rifle ammunition. On the long journey the gentle stamping and eating noises of the horses were an obligato to my memories, lived over repeatedly in the swaying car.

I recalled there was one fence post down the road by our ranch which caught the eye each spring morning, for, year after year, a meadowlark made it a stage for her daily concert.

And Roscoe Bean's funeral procession with lumber wagons, a few buggies and surreys, and many on horseback, nearly half a mile long, when we buried him in the arid cemetery overgrown with Russian thistles and other aggressive weeds—Roscoe, the best of the best.

There was also my stepmother, by the oil lamp in the kitchen, reading aloud some long book like *The Cloister and the Hearth*, or a novel by Ralph Connor, *The Man from Glengarry* or *The Sky Pilot,* while outside the whisper and hiss of the snow as it cascaded over our valley. Hired men, chairs propped against the walls, smoked their pipes and listened, or the bearded one snored softly, which no one minded. Cats and dogs were at ease beneath the table.

I had much to recall—skating on the big pond in winter,

and the handsome girls, and the sun-blasted wooden ranch shacks, each year a darker color; in summer, the sharp lines of separation between the desert and the sown, and the glint of mica as one drank from the warm flow in irrigation ditches; in spring, the perfume of orchards in the time of flowering; and, in autumn, a deep pride in stacks of alfalfa of over one hundred tons standing against the sky, the fruit of long days.

There was the tall figure of the old prospector whose ledge of lead-silver galena ore away to the north, so long ago located and now lost, which beckoned to him each summer until he perished in the quest.

And Don Meek's voice as he sat beneath a giant spruce up on Black Mesa, rain falling softly, dripping from his battered hat, sharing with us boys what life had given him, raising questions for himself, and us, which none of us could answer, kindly, a terrible fighter when necessary, but a man of peace nevertheless, as he peered into the darkness of man's ignorance and need, with eyes more keen than we possessed.

Except for the sage which always kept its shades of grey, autumn brought vivid yellows in the North Carolina and Lombardy poplars and cottonwoods that some ranchers away down the valley had planted along the ditches. Milder browns came in orchards and tawny patches in fields as greens retreated before winter's coming. On distant mountains saffron appeared where aspen forests alternated with evergreens, and, with the turning of the seasons, the Northern Lights.

There was much to remember as the freight train roared over the Oregon Short Line past Pocatello and on down to Provo and Salt Lake, and east on the Denver and Rio Grande toward Green River and Colorado. My thoughts ran around in my head like a squirrel in a cage, always returning to neighbors and the family, for I knew this was a final break. "When I was a child I thought as a child." In the next chapter of life I had to think as a grown-up.

I thought much about our neighbors. A mixture of

dreams and sharp reality was in their minds and hearts. A settler living in a meager shack would point a scarred and horny hand at a stretch of sagebrush and say, "When I get on my feet we will build the new house there," or, "We intend to raise only pure Herefords." Dreams were seldom realized, but deeply cherished. Our neighbors saw things as they were, bargained hard, never suffered fools gladly, despised the boaster. Dreamers can also be realists. In recurrent hardships they did not panic. No darkness of night, blackness of pain or failure, could last forever among these people; no hard times smother their hope; no sorrow or loss dim their faith in the land, no weariness arrest their feet. They were made to sweat it out. Suns of July and August baked all nonsense out of them. Deep frosts of winter forced them to contract within themselves, hard and self-reliant.

And they could laugh, these people! These were not only belly laughs at antics of children and animals, and humorous sallies at friend and neighbor, they could laugh at hardship and even tragedy. A poor man loses his best horse, a rancher just getting out of debt has his haystack burn—they could still laugh! There was no merriment in this, and no bitterness. It was their armor against yielding to defeat, their *Invictus* flung against the totality of life and loss and death.

What had our neighbors been like, inside, deep inside? Often I had deceived myself by overquick judgments about schoolmates and adults. As I had listenened to older people talk, often sharply and critically, of one another they seemed to divide up neighbors in many different ways. All methods made some sense, but none completely satisfied.

Some neighbors separated people neatly into the good and the bad. But there were few I knew who were wholly good, and almost none entirely bad. Some divided humanity into the generous and the stingy. The openhanded were easy enough to locate; the stingy were those who refused to help build the Valley View schoolhouse, or to aid when the poor family were burnt out. Others divided men into the lazy and the hard workers. We could see this plainly, every day, along our road.

Then, some made the division along lines of the weak and the strong. Well, certainly the weak were trampled on like the poor Englishman at Falk's Store. A man was lucky to have power to defend himself. The weak seemed to invite cruelty upon themselves, like a chicken, caught in the wire, draws upon himself other seemingly docile chickens who proceed to pick him to death. The strong like the orangutan nephew at Falk's Store who brutally beat up the helpless stranger, need visible and immediate curbs.

And some divided men into those friendly and those unfriendly. The friendly were certainly like the French family, helpful and gracious, always lending a hand. And the unfriendly were like those reluctant to help. Sometimes men were in one group, sometimes in another.

Lying on the hay as the boxcar lurched along I thought much about the different sorts of people. As I saw it, none of these divisions into which our neighbors divided one another was always airtight. When you put pigs in a pen you thought was fool proof, they still someway escaped. People were like that. They did not stay forever in the same pen. Our neighbors were a mixture. They varied in what they said, or did, from day to day, or hour to hour, as to whether they had a good breakfast, sold hay at a profit, made a good horse trade, whether the wife was good-natured, whether children jumped in to help or dragged their feet. It looked as if in the valley we were about a mill run of the human race.

It was fairly obvious that no one is of one piece, all the time, nor were there any, or very few, with completely single motives. It appeared that one could only judge what a man is at the one moment in question, although his general attitude cannot be overlooked.

But was it unfair for a man to dislike being ineffectual, a failure? Was it not commendable to desire success? It seemed to me hatred of defeat was natural and praiseworthy, and to wish and to work for success was normal. Defeat and success could lie in many fields other than in money alone or in owning a good ranch free of debt.

As I tried to add up our neighbors I felt that most of them, whatever were their unpleasant habits or repeated failures, whether they were free of debt, or loaded with unpayable mortgages, whether their families were stable or jangled, if they had a strong desire not to be useless but to ring up some successes, they were on the right track.

One night, listening to the roar of the train, I tried to weigh up myself. What did others think of me, the ones who knew me best? I shied away from that, I dimly saw I was inclined to escape difficulties of hard thinking by grabbing near opportunities for action. But then, one was what one was. If I was to change entirely, I would not be myself.

Our minister saw few boys during good weather for then we were working on the crops, but he often visited us in the fields. I tried to remember some of these visits and what he had said, for at such times we could exchange ideas not possible in formal services.

"You must be born again," he had said, "you must 'put on the new man.' You don't even have to be successful, but you should try. You do have to live among all sorts of people, you must give them a break, and you have to work, hard. Know when you do wrong, and don't fool yourself about it. If you lie, go and apologize. If you steal, and I know all of you have, pay back more than you stole. And don't worry too much about little things, especially about occasional failures. You won't be worth a damn if you can always keep up with your ideals. Don't cry over spilt milk! The perfect chance to do the perfect thing will never come. Even repentence can be a vice. Get up each day and start over again. The big thing is what you intend to do. What you do do is so often conditioned by others. Be free, inside, and keep going. Your big job is to be a man. It is possible to be a success in the eyes of the world, and still not be a real man. And the opposite is true. Being born again is a matter of the intent of your heart."

The minister did not have that variety of kindness which,

however genuine, appears apologetic. Kind, he was, but never soft. It is easy to make fun of Protestant ministers, there is an open season on them all year around, but no one could make fun of him. He had been a farmer, his hands calloused from plow and axe, his mind hard and clear, with an inclusive love for all in the community, willing to serve the meanest of us but never tempering his austere judgments to gain an easy popularity. He was the stuff of the old-fashioned circuit rider. He often worked at day labor on the ranches doing any job as well as the best. We all recognized he was a man; he respected himself, and us, and he respected his office, his task as a clergyman. He asked the same of us, and he got it.

He looked us in the eye and spoke truth as he saw it. "Don't expect something for nothing. 'Nothing for nothing, and very little for a sixpence is the rule of life!' Don't spend more than you make. Do your share, don't whine, lend a hand. Don't eat your morsel alone. No one owes you anything. You have life and health, and that is enough. You'll never know how to command until you learn how to obey." Perhaps all of us recalled some of his proverbs, "He who will not listen to the rudder, must need listen to the rock!" "You can't make a whistle out of a pig's tail, nor a silk purse out of a sow's ear!" He put it on the line, without apology.

The schoolmaster, too, had said things I recalled. All of us had respected him for he had put his back into the job. "You want to have a good reputation, don't you? Well, the chances are if you set out directly to get it, you'll lose it, for you may lie and cheat to make an impression. Most of us do that. A good name is rather a by-product of doing well. Forget it! Keep plugging, and a good reputation will come. If you want to rise above the herd—and you should —then make a harder demand upon yourself than others make upon themselves."

He once told us the story of Cervante's *Don Quixote,* which he was reading. The old Don had said to his servant, "Take note, Brother Sancho, that no man is better than another, unless he does better!" That stuck in our craws! Like the teacher we had had in Dry Gulch school in Colorado, and the minister, our Idaho schoolmaster was great on proverbs. On this business of doing good work, one day he quoted, "Seest thou a man diligent in his business, he shall stand before kings!"

Well, I could go along with these ideas! No need for me to worry about what the neighbors thought of me, for now that I was leaving, I could not change my record along our road.

One long night the horses were restless. I rolled out of my blankets to brush them down, speak to them, give them a little feed, arrange the bedding, a half bucket of water each, and to adjust the halters, which did not need it. Horses are like fidgety little children, at certain moments doing some useless thing for them brings comfort, and they settle down. I talked aloud and sometimes sang to them which seemed to bring steadiness.

The boxcar rumbled through cuts and over bridges, the locomotive whistle echoed like music through Utah's canyons as the wheels clicked over rails leading to the high valley in Colorado, and I decided our neighbors in the Payette Valley were good people and that I was lucky to have lived with them.

During the long stop in Salt Lake City I gave a boy two bits to stay with the horses while I took a trolley ride up in the town. I laid in some more grub, bought several bottles of strawberry, lemon sour and cream soda pop, a couple of packets of Duke's Mixture, and revisited the fine Mormon buildings.

Trainmen rode with me quite often and as I fed them from what I had provided, they would spot the boxcar where I could more easily refill my barrels with water. Hobos several times accompanied me long distances, two sleeping on the hay on the leg between Pocatello and Provo; them also I fed. I could not give the men coffee as I dared not use any heating device but once a brakeman brought a bucketful from the caboose. They had interesting yarns, those hobos, and they helped me in cleaning up after the horses. I never had any trouble with them, and I liked these free spirits who roamed the earth as birds of passage.

My boxcar became a place of rendezvous for both trainmen and hobos, the two fraternizing on equal terms. On a night run in eastern Utah one mare, weary with bracing herself against the swaying of the train, lay down. When she sought to get up at a stop she was unable to do so. Both trainmen and hobos helped me get her on her feet. Her shoes had not been removed as had been done with some of the horses and I feared she might, in floundering about, injure herself or others. Toward morning when we stopped by an icing station for refrigerator cars, the hobos and I swiped a lot of sawdust to help make a better bedding for the horses. The sawdust absorbed the wet and was easy to clean up.

Now I was a man, or trying to become one. I was seventeen and a half. What had my years taught? Experience assured that if I kept at it I might not gain exactly what I wished, but often something better. Clearing land taught that every stroke of the axe counted.

A lively appreciation of those who had helped did something for me, inside. There had been so many who had lent a hand—parents, teachers, sisters, two ministers, my stepmother, and the boys with whom I had learned and worked and played and fought.

I had memories nothing could take away, the fierce pleasure, pride if you will, of putting raw land beneath the plow, of making earth produce which had never borne a crop, recollections of friends, old and young, schoolmates, hired men, memories of the land, of horses, cows, colts, calves, and little animals.

Life had taught that almost anything was possible to a family like the Meehans who hung together and helped one another, or to a group like those along our road which built the Valley View school, with nary a thought of asking help from Boise or Washington.

Most of us boys, and girls as well, had to miss long periods at school to work in planting and harvesting. We learned that early rising was the only way we could get in both necessary home studies and the ranch work. There was an old cowboy saying whose truth we accepted. "He who rises late shall trot all day." Life had been good, very good, so far.

Life taught also there was no substitute for self-reliance, to hold on, to bend and not to break. And I had learned that complaint was useless, that most suffering was self-caused, as the Dunkard girl had said. The deserter from the German army who had been in the Boxer Uprising, had told me of a Chinese proverb. "I had no shoes and I complained, until I met a man without feet!" That, too, made sense.

The smell of a sweaty horse, one whiff of sage, recall the good ranch life, sunsets over Oregon at the close of a hard day's plowing, gray, brush-clad hills, Squaw Butte blurred and wavy in August heat, blue smudges on the Seven Devils Mountains where forests lay below timberline, the steamy breath of alfalfa fields under irrigation, neighing of colts, voices of turtledoves in the cottonwoods, the quiet comfort of horses eating in the night. The years had taught that there was much to bear in life, but that life was to be loved and lived.

The big thing was to do one's part, not to hang back, to be a volunteer. Be jubilant my feet!